ZEPHYR
of Time

What then is time?
If no one ask me, I know what it is.
If I wish to explain it to him who asks,
I do not know.

~ St. Augustine, *Confessions, Book 11* ~

ALSO BY JOSEPH COLWELL

Canyon Breezes:
Exploring Magical Places in Nature

ZEPHYR
of Time

Meditations on Time and Nature

JOSEPH COLWELL

Norm Best wishes to a good California friend. Joseph Colwell Nov. 2017

Lichen Rock Press
Hotchkiss, Colorado 81419

Editing: Laura Duggan
Design and publishing services: Constance King Design
Cover photographs and illustrations: Katherine Colwell

Front cover, top: full lunar eclipse—the "Blood Moon" rising over
Mt. Lamborn, September 27, 2015, as seen from Colwell Cedars Retreat,
Delta County, Colorado.
Front cover, bottom: sunset as seen from Colwell Cedars Retreat.

Lichen Rock Press
Hotchkiss, Colorado
ColwellCedars.com

ISBN: 978-0-9962222-1-1
Printed in USA

Author's Invitation

*Imagination is everything. It is the preview
of life's coming attraction.*

~ Albert Einstein ~

A zephyr is a gentle breeze, a mild west wind. I grew up
in Illinois and that will always be home to me, although I
left it at the age of 18. The zephyr from the West pulled me
and the West has claimed me since. The zephyr drew me
into my future, but it can also take me home into the past.
The wind, a constant throughout time, has helped shape the
West I love and find intriguing in its exposure of the distant
past. Mountains, deserts, canyons, seashores—all shaped by
the wind, have a story to tell if we only care to listen.

The question 'what is time?' has intrigued me for much
of my life. As the days and years added up to a lifetime of
searching, the intrigue turned to haunt. We all are limited
in our search and none of us knows how much time we
have. My sense of urgency increases as my clock of days
runs towards its inevitable end.

Several people have told me that I think too much. I plead
guilty. I ask questions about everything. My curiosity has
searched the ends of the universe and the beginnings of
time. I ask questions no one can answer.

The past also haunts me. I missed out on most of this
history of this planet. So I wonder about the old days,
those days that came and went without me. They are
important because they created what I am seeing now.

We mistakenly believe that we cannot change the past; we can, but we do not know how. My theory of time is that it is all interwoven, switching back and forth from past to future at will. But until we know how time really works, my questions still continue to absorb me. What did the passenger pigeons see and what did the last one think about? What were my ancestors like and what kind of world did they think they would leave me? I will always be tugged by that zephyr of time to go back, to go home. I explore these and many more questions, searching, wondering.

The opening essay is entitled *Zephyr of Time.* To me, the concept of time is like the wind. It is ephemeral, yet persistent. We cannot grasp the meaning of the wind nor can we grasp the meaning of time. To me they are the same. We wish to ride on one, and go back to visit the other. Neither can happen, but we spend countless hours dreaming about the possibilities. Join me in my search for meanings in nature and time.

Joseph Colwell, March 30, 2016
Hotchkiss, Colorado

CONTENTS

THE UNIVERSE OF TIME

*The illimitable, silent, never-resting thing called Time,
rolling, rushing on, swift, silent, like an
all-embracing ocean-tide, on which we and all the
universe swim like exhalations, like apparitions
which are, and then are not....*

~ Thomas Carlyle, *On Heroes and Hero Worship* ~

ZEPHYR OF TIME

A gentle west wind is called a zephyr, an ancient word, coming first from Greek, then Latin, meaning darkness and west. The aboriginal peoples saw west as dark, the color blue or black in their cycle of life and its circle of light. It is where the sun sets and where darkness deepens as the last trace of sunlight disappears into the blue black of night. A wind coming from the west, especially the West I am familiar with, the Rocky Mountains, is the default wind, the normal wind that carries the monotonous passage of time. Southwesterly or northwesterly winds often bring storms, rain, snow, and a break from the drift of time. To me, the wind, especially the west wind, is symbolic of time, that mystery of life that advances steadily onward, beyond our power to understand or control.

Time is something as steady and reliable as the west wind, a gentle breeze, a zephyr. It is irreversible. The zephyr, like the passage of time, is steady, an irresistible force, reminding us of gentler times, irreplaceable memories, happiness as well as sadness, nostalgia for something that is gone forever. That breeze that gently passed us by, carrying the scent of cherry blossoms and lilacs, can never occur again. Other breezes may be similar, but never exactly the same. Time, that accompanies the gentle west wind, its sights and sounds, scents and memories, will also never carry events again exactly as they once were.

We try to understand what time is. Philosophers, sages, shamans, priests, commoners alike, throughout the long span of time that we wandered asking questions of the night sky, have all failed to understand what time is. It is as elusive as trying to see the wind. We can feel the zephyr, as we can feel the aging that time does to our minds and bodies. We cannot see the wind, nor can we see time. But we can see, feel, hear what it does. The west wind called to the early trappers and explorers seeking wealth of fur and adventure, to the California Argonauts of '49 seeking the golden fleece of riches, even to the Europeans seeking the freedom and wealth from a new world. In the same way, the search for the fountain of youth, that elixir that erases the ravages of time, has claimed even more seekers, eagerly looking for that lost wealth of youth.

We can no more find the way to turn back time than we can find the source of that west wind. We can stand on a mountaintop or a seashore and face the wind, but it will never tell us its source. The wind is limitless as is time, though the years and hours of time to any one of us mortals does have a limit. We mourn for the time that has gone behind us as we drifted with our own gentle winds of life. We think the past could have been different, gentler, more generous. But we all know it is a game of fools to face into those winds. What is past has passed. Neither a new beginning nor a forgotten time can be found.

Zephyrs carried the sands of long eroded mountain ranges across vast deserts, then dropped them into the depths of seas since turned to stone by time unimagined.

Over the eons, they continue as if they were still new born on the land. They continue on while the time they have seen is gone as well. Just as the future is time waiting to turn into the past, the west winds are a gentle reminder that we are just passing time, waiting for our turn to drift over the vast seas and the vast eons of time.

Is it all meaningless? Just as time past can teach us the mysteries that evade the wisest of us, the wind can teach us patience and the wisdom we seek. The raven and the eagle use the breeze to soar and play, catching thermals and downdrafts. The fire catches the wind to bring new growth to the forests and grasslands. If we can learn to float with the wind, maybe we can someday find that secret to go back in time.

We anticipate the future, dream of what we will become, what might happen without traveling into the future. But the past is where unmet dreams are left wanting. The choices not made, the errors of our judgement, the miscarriage of fate, all lie in the past, haunting us with the 'what ifs' of life. The joys of dreams met, the nostalgia of our youth, the successes we enjoyed, all lie in the past. We dream of going back to enjoy them all again, but can never do so. They have blown past us like the wind, a breeze that we can feel but never grab onto and hold. The future arrives, and is immediately the past. There is no present. The future is anticipated, but we cannot grab onto the wind, and we cannot hold onto the present.

Thus we must enjoy that gentle breeze on our face as we turn into the wind and smile at what has left us behind. Our lives move on, just as surely as that west wind, a zephyr of memories and smiles, will continue to pass us by on its search for the future.

Who Owns Time?

In late 1990, on a cold winter day, my wife and I signed papers that documented our ownership of forty acres in Western Colorado. We had been searching for a place in which to move after I retired about a dozen years from then. The land was an old homestead, vacated only two years previously by Hazel, a hermit recluse who had lived here for at least fifty years. A long journey started for us that snowy day and is still progressing in our trip through time.

The property was exactly what we were looking for. It was mostly forested, although with juniper and a few piñon and not the higher elevation aspen and spruce that I would have preferred. It had views to live for—of the distant San Juan Mountains, the West Elk Mountains, the North Fork Valley below us, the Black Canyon of the Gunnison across the valley. Year-round spring-fed streams filled two draws with cattails and wetlands, which enhanced the excellent wildlife habitat.

In the ensuing years, we learned many things, the most important of which is that we do not own the land. It owns us. We are temporary tenants, caretakers, living with many other inhabitants, sharing a world that is as old as time itself. As if it mattered, we can easily trace ownership of this piece of land. We bought it from a speculator who owned it less than a month. He nearly doubled his investment in that short time. He realized this piece of land held a value not understood by most people. He had purchased it from three young ladies who had inherited it three years earlier from their childless aunt Hazel, the hermit recluse. Hazel had obtained title from the U.S. Government via the Homestead Act in 1940. The government had obtained title when it forced the previous owners off their land in the late 19th century and proclaimed itself owner. The Utes, or Nuche, had "owned" it for untold millennia prior to that, although they fully understood they didn't own anything. They were semi-nomadic and lived as part of this land, one of many owners, including the trees, the deer, the mountain lion, the eagle. They knew you could no more own the land, the animals, the clouds, as you could own time. The land was time and it had no beginning or end.

As I now care for the land, tending and restoring the damage done by overgrazing, littering, cutting of trees, all of which destroyed native plants and animals, I realize what the Nuche and their ancestors knew instinctively. The land is sacred and we use it with permission of all other life forms. The frog down in the pond, the gopher snake slithering over the rocks, the ravens and eagles overhead, the ancient junipers, the sagebrush, the sego lilies, the cactus, the lichens covering the rocks, all own this place they together call home.

The land is time, which like life itself is forever changing. As an ecologist, I understand that nature does not stay the same. A person may want to live in a place with a nice view of a forested hillside or a peaceful lake. But the forested hillside will change. Fire or disease will inevitably reduce the trees to skeletons. The lake will fill in to become a meadow. A herd of deer that frequent the winter landscape may move on to greener pastures or change their migration pattern. The scenery changes, and so does the land itself.

The forty acres that I now enjoy were something else
not that long ago, but for my meager lifespan, I can count
on them not changing significantly. But change occurs.
When glaciers had finished picking off the edges of Grand
Mesa and depositing the black basalt boulders on the
ice which then left it on my property, the melting water
scoured the hillsides, creating a huge lake below me. The
scene I now view as orchards and pastures below my
mesa was once a happening place as glacial floodwaters
churned and left deposits of gravel and boulders. A few
eons before that, the remains of a Mediterranean-like sea
left thousands of feet of what turned into shale, covering
the landscape with a sterile badlands. And for millions of
years prior to that, the sands and muds and sea sediment
were solidifying into rock that is carved into the Colorado
Plateau as a wonderland of canyons and cliffs today.

At one time dinosaurs roamed and bellowed exactly
where my house now stands. Then at another time, that
vast sea covered my bedroom to an unknown depth. I am
guardian of all that. I watch over the spirits of those beasts,
the energy that still vibrates from the atoms that built
their cells that may still float through the mountain air I
breathe. How can I ignore the very time that helps make
the land what it is today?

It is the dream of many people to own their own home.
They may own a small piece of land in a town or city,
squeezed between a hundred or a thousand other houses,
all unaware of what happened on that land more than
a couple hundred years earlier. But the history is there,
hidden beneath the asphalt and concrete and wooden
walls. The spirits are lost as is the connection with all
other living things.

Here, though, I can feel the energy. I wander like a

child awed by the mystery of the world surrounding him. I am a visitor who wishes to understand the cry of the raven, to talk to the deer staring at me with those large liquid brown eyes. They wonder about me like I wonder about them. They, and those like them that lived here before my human ancestors, who learned to utter those first words that took us on a separate journey long, long ago, own this land. I am here with their permission. Yet humans act as if our feathered and four legged relatives don't belong except as something that we allow.

I wish to go back in time when the sea lapped the shores of a distant land beyond sight over the eastern horizon. There were no mountains then. They had long ago been reduced to the mud that sank below me to form a shale that grew to a great depth. I want to hover above the water, green and blue, reflecting clouds that have formed and dissolved and reformed a thousand million times since then. What strange sea birds flew over this ocean and what fish probed the depths? Or was there life at all other than blue green algae?

Or take me back further to when my land sat on the edge of a huge Sahara-like Desert, with endless red sand dunes stretching to the setting sun. The land was red, the sky was red, the clouds were red. Where my chipmunks now scamper, there was no hint of life of any kind.

The days were all the same since my land was sitting near the equator, that chunk of land now called North America part of a land mass long ago split asunder and set in motion across the world. It was indeed a different world. But I own that, too. Where does my land title say that? Where I now look out my bedroom window and see a distant line of white peaks reaching towards the moon, at one time that lump of rising land was awash with lava and belching steam. Calderas the size of Yellowstone were building new land and creating what I see as a wilderness of high peaks and plateaus and canyons, full of flowers and elk and grizzly, until a century and a half ago when we destroyed the Garden of Eden that existed. What landowner carries that burden of guilt for what we did to that creation of wonder? I claim innocence yet I still bear the responsibility. Can I buy what that paradise looked like when the Nuche wandered its canyons and rivers?

I want to go back, but the only direction I am allowed to go is forward and I can only apologize to the future landowners for what I did and didn't do. My kind in my time were poor landlords and someday, we will be ashamed, but not now. We are too shortsighted and too greedy to care or even realize what we own. We own time whether or not we understand what that means. I own the dinosaur bones hidden deep under my feet. I own the raindrops that fell a million years ago, now trapped in the sandstone a mile beneath me. I own the sky all the way to the moon and beyond. Where does it stop? Do I own a piece of Mars? Or will someone in the future destroy that for their descendants to inherit?

No, I don't own anything. Nor does anyone else. We are visitors who deserve eviction, but who will kick us out? Someone will. Maybe a virus or a bacteria or the sky and polluted water itself.

I look at the piece of paper that says this is all mine. I will treat the land as if it actually is mine, with the permission of the badger that sits outside the gate, with the cooperation of the dragonfly that has flown these skies for longer than the land has been here. I will sit on a rock and sing along with the meadowlark that welcomes each spring morning with song. And sing with the frogs that

serenade the night sky, that same sky that glowed red with
the volcanoes of ages past. We all own it now and we own
the past, but we also own the future. And what will that
be? Every morning as I greet the sun with a humble thank
you, I know that I am not only home, but I will forever
be coming home. The morning dew welcomes me with
a refreshing purity that is new each day. I will continue
to come home until someday, I will be a part of this, just
like the black lichen covered boulders and the breeze that
ruffles the tree tops and shakes the dew off the flowers.

Blowing in the Winds

The wind is as elusive as time, and has blown as long as time has sped through the universe. The winds have many faces and twice as many personalities. We each have memories of winds throughout our time of life.

I have stood on mountain tops and seashores, on the endless grass ocean of the Great Plains and the shifting patterns of desert sands. The biting blizzards of January shooting stinging snow pellets into my frozen face contrast to the gentle summer breezes wafting puffy cottonball clouds across a blue sky. The never-ending winds of the high plains have been as ruthless as the downdrafts from the gunmetal blue-grey of the towering desert thunderstorms.

And what is the wind? I have studied the science of the change in atmospheric pressure which causes the winds and have shaken my head at the mystery that still exists. Science does not delve into the emotions that winds can cause nor does it explain that wind is really nothing at all. You cannot see it unless it carries snow or rain or dust as a free riding companion. But you feel it, and you sense the history it carries.

Katherine and I were walking a trail in Theodore Roosevelt National Park in North Dakota. We were a mile from the truck and lost in an expanse of prairie grass that waved in a gentle west wind. As we stood breathing the air of a wild freedom, we saw a herd of bison walking out of a swale a mile ahead of us. They kept coming in a wavering line, intent on what bison do. We were downwind and two small humans obviously were of little interest to them. They surely saw us, but in this wide expanse, they ignored our presence. At least that was what I was hoping as they stopped to graze, then slowly turned towards us. It was time we turned slowly and headed in that same direction—towards the safety of our vehicle.

It didn't occur to me at that time, since my primeval fear of being alone without cover as these huge beasts lumbered towards us overruled any philosophical thoughts, but I had immediately been thrust back thousands of years. I was breathing the same air of twenty or fifty thousand years ago, seeing the same view as the ancestors of these magnificent animals (vegetarians by the way) saw, minus a huge continental ice sheet not too far over the northern horizon. Other than the clothes we wore, we were alone with the elements that existed millennia ago when mastodon shared these plains with saber tooth cats, giant ground sloths, and giant bison, all now relegated to archeologic digs and fossil beds. The breeze blew unceasingly as it did long ago, only now not quite as pure.

Decades ago, we were on a pack trip high on the tundra plateau of Colorado's southern San Juan Mountains, southwest of the headwaters of the Rio Grande. I was new enough to the mountains and to my Forest Service job of checking out the high country sheep range, that I didn't factor in the daily afternoon thunderstorms. We had topped timberline and were winding our way through the krumholtz, that stunted bonsai-like effort of trees to exist higher in elevation than they should. The growing thunderheads blew in from the southwest and hit us like

a hammer. The winds led the way, herding the lightning
and thunder. The wind howled, slamming rain and hail
into our faces as we slid off the horses, not even bothering
to tie them to a stunted tree. They were on their own, as
were we. The lightning flashed all around us as we tried
to dig our way into the ground, soon covered by hail.
Thunder accompanied the lightning within a split second.
Once again, other than our nylon rain slickers and the
fancy saddles and ropes of our horses, we could have
been huddling here a thousand years before. This was
nature in the raw, untamed by time and civilization. As
the clouds splintered and feathered, the winds died down.
The sun came out to apologize for the fit of rain and wind.
We caught the horses, who seemed to be oblivious to the
turmoil they just passed through, and life continued on
in the pristine tundra of the continental divide of extreme
southern Colorado. Only years later did we learn that
the last confirmed grizzly in Colorado roamed these very
meadows and forests. We breathed the same air as did griz
and his forebears, their scent and energy still hovering
over the plateau. Winds do not always scour out the air.
They sometimes bounce off the energy of forces more
powerful than the breeze.

Walking through the slickrock canyons and deserts
of Utah, I was always amazed at the artistry of the wind.
It was not only the wind sculpted sandstone, showing the
swirls and dunes of long petrified sand, but the current
swirls and circles of wind-blown stems of grass in the
sandy soil. A lonely stem of ricegrass, struggling to survive
in this harsh environment, would be turned this way and
that by changing winds, leaving a circle etched into the
sand. Then tracks of a mouse or chipmunk would pitter
patter along a soft and smooth section of sandy soil,

protected by a rock overhang, leaving his prints until a more powerful wind would smooth it like an etch-a-sketch. The winds seemed ceaseless in the desert, carrying echoes that bounced it along with the aria of the canyon wren singing hidden in the canyons. That haunting echo became more powerful as the wind ceased at night, only to pick up again as the cooling air fell down from the nearby mountain heights, creating a cool breeze that made a campfire of piñon branches the more comforting.

The winds bring the rain and snow that allow life. Winds sculpt the rock, move dunes back and forth, awaiting the day they can turn into rock. But the wind does not blow all the time. What happens when the winds stop? Does time stop as well? The lack of wind allows me to catch my breath, to feel the earth as it inhales for its next exhalation. The quiet frozen air of a deep winter day, in its stillness, creates the diamonds of sunshine floating off the snowy landscape. The slowly rising heated air of the desert blast furnace creates mirages and dancing visions of fairies present only in the hazy blue sky. These dog days of quiet windless times allow me to regroup, to guess at the dance of the winds, whether they return as blizzards, howling sandstorms, or thunderstorms full of fury and motion.

I relate wind to time. Just as the cosmic wind, carrying photons and ions at the speed of light crossing the vacuum of space carry no time with them, the winds that hit our face as we sit on this revolving planet, far short of the speed of light, take us back in time. Every particle that hits us, carried by that mysterious breeze of dust and air, carries with it the history of all the winds that have caressed the surface of the earth. For the wind carries atoms and molecules, carbon and oxygen, that once were part of dinosaurs, ancient ginkgo trees, mastodons and Greek philosophers. The wind, the very air we breathe, is the history of the earth. We need only listen to the rustle of the leaves, the swaying of the grass, the raindrops falling with the wind from the cloud tops to hear that history.

The sunlight is the new energy coming from a star, the creation of life, the future of us all. But the wind is our history, our past. It carries the wisdom of all life before us. It tells a story if we only care to listen. As we sit on the sea coast, a mountain top, a grassy expanse of plains, a rocky canyon, a swamp forming the coal of a distant future—we sit in their classrooms. Let the breeze tousle your hair, fill your lungs, carry you back to earlier days. A breeze carries memories, a time from our past. Close your eyes and let it take you there.

TIME

A few years after his ninetieth birthday, my father, never one to seek or embrace new ideas or philosophies, asked me what time was. Not what time it was at that moment of the evening, since his life had already evolved into a routine of simplicity, but what the concept of time involved. How could I answer that? What could he understand or grasp in the twilight years of a long life that witnessed such advances in technology and lifestyle?

I had spent countless hours contemplating this very subject, confusing myself beyond all imagination. Submerging myself into the weirdness of quantum physics, Einstein, parallel universes, time travel, and the fourth dimension, I had molded all the differing versions of time that I studied into my own personal definition of time. I came to the conclusion that the concept of time was much like the concept of religion or a person's own spiritual beliefs. The cornerstone of this was the fact that no one on earth really understood what time was, thus there was no answer, no right or wrong, nothing too weird. That is the type of science I like. No equations—although I'm confident some mathematician could come up with something (using advanced calculus I'm sure)—no formulas, no proofs and no complicated studies. Just pure and personal speculation.

I tried to tell my father that time was relative. A light beam, going the speed of light, involved no time whatsoever. A supernova blew out photons that had traveled billions of years across the universe before they smashed into his eyes as he watched the twinkling starlight on a dark November night while stumbling through a riverbank forest on a routine coon hunt. Yet if he had somehow managed to hitch a ride on that photon, his departure from the star and his arrival in the night sky of an Illinois winter would be instantaneous. He would not have aged a second. There is no passage of time for starbeams. The expanding universe, as it measures itself on a speeding photon, has not passed one second of time since its creation from the Big Bang. How, then, can we say it is 15 billion years old? It is still in the cradle of infancy. I cannot even grasp that meaning myself. I knew he couldn't either.

For us earthlings plodding along in our mundane lives, time passes slowly at some times, then quickly at others. We have fooled ourselves into thinking we know about time since we can measure it. But why is it that my first memory on this earth—some sixty-odd years ago preschool day hanging onto the windmill at Ervin Morgan's farm outside Tuscola, Illinois—seems like yesterday, but I cannot remember what I did at 9 am three days ago? Time is not the memories we hold onto as well as forget. The memories are there, representing time, but they are not time. If I forget them, well, that is a fault with my brain, not with any ravages of time.

Look at old photographs. They represent time at one instant. We captured time, we held onto it, froze it, and stopped it. Think back to that moment the camera shutter clicked, back in the days when there were shutters and they actually clicked shut. I can go back in time and remember what I was doing, feel the emotions, smell the odors, feel the warmth of the sun or the breeze in the air. That is true time travel. But again, we are only reigniting neurons. We aren't traveling back in time. Or are we?

Time is relative in the sense that if I travel on a new road, especially a winding rocky road on some lonely mountain, it takes forever and a day, even if the clock says it was one hour. The second time I travel that same road under the same conditions, it didn't take long after all. That is relativity. Sitting in an uncomfortable chair listening to some boring lecture slows time down to a standstill. Watching an engrossing and exciting movie or dancing with a beautiful young lady on a college date, time speeds up to nearly the speed of light. The happy moment is over just as it got started, the unhappy moment lasts forever. That is relativity even my father can understand. The relativity of Einstein? It may be a different concept, but we get the point. 'It all depends' is an answer that comes in handy on many different occasions.

I could have tried to tell my father that time is a circle, just like life itself. We are born the second we die. Only we don't die; we jump in time. We can jump forward or backward. We can go back and stand next to a sleeping mastodon on an endless prairie, or hide in the jungle as stegosauri wander by, trumpeting their passage. Or end up next to whatever species replaces humans at some distance place in the future, a future when the memory of humans is as distant as our memory (or knowledge) of dinosaurs.

Time is not an arrow as many scientists claim. They whip out equations and experiments that prove to them that time is one way and what is past has passed and will reoccur nevermore. Some things we have to take on faith. Such as faith itself. We have no problem believing that God is hiding up there in the clouds. Maybe he is; maybe she is joyriding around the universe on starbeams, passing no time at all.

It may have taken him over ninety years, but my

father was starting to ask questions I had been dealing with for years. Time had taken more of a toll on him than me. After all, I have always remembered television and telephones, automobiles and airplanes. He was born when Teddy Roosevelt was president. His father was born when Abe Lincoln was alive. How could I even comprehend the changes that time and technology had presented him? It wouldn't be very many years before he started his time travel. I envied him. He would soon know what time was as he hops on that merry-go-round that is the time (or lack of time) that we can only guess about now.

What is time, he asked? It is the past, the present, the future, all at once, intertwined, interchangeable. The future can influence the past, the present doesn't have to follow the past or influence the future. "Come again?" I can hear him respond to a statement I don't dare speak to him. I cannot explain it; he cannot understand it. To travel in time and explore its wonders, you have to be open to something approximating reincarnation, but that's not really correct either. It's energy, but then explaining and understanding energy is just as difficult as the concept of time. And time, of course, is energy, or at least a component of it. He didn't ask me about energy, and who am I to try and bring that up to someone whose simple pleasures of life have settled into watching reruns of Lawrence Welk, and University of Illinois basketball games. Why confuse things at this point in life, I thought, as I changed the subject. Time, I said, was something God understood, but hadn't let us in on the secret yet. I think maybe he understood that. But his smile made me realize he knew better. Maybe I should have asked him what time was. He probably wouldn't have told me either. Maybe he was just testing me.

MIRACLES ON A
TIMELESS SEASHORE

I have visited an ocean coast not more than a dozen times in my life. Although I am drawn to the seashore and the crashing waves on rocky headlands, I keep these experiences rare. Part of it is due to my home, cradled in the inland mountains, vast expanses of a different kind. But part is a justification I make. Too much of a good thing lessens its value. The visits become special, a chance to reflect and contemplate that cannot be found in the boredom of familiarity.

As I stand on the beach or the rock sculptured cliffs, mesmerized by the ceaseless waves, the vast water spread before me to an unknown horizon, I believe that time has indeed stopped. "Timeless, endless, infinite, forever"—the words all mean the same in my mind. The oceans have humbled explorers since ships first sailed the seas. The waters seemed to hide distant lands in mystery. They put a boundary to our knowledge and our existence. But they were there and had been forever. How could such an enduring miracle of space and motion not be there forever?

But the seas define time. Time is our past, our present, our future. We are time and we are the universe. We are all there is and all we will ever know. When I sit on the cliffs above the seashore and watch the gulls soar and scream as they search for their daily meal, I thank the waves for bringing a mystery to crash on the shore. I marvel at the clouds, painting the sky white, orange, lavender, blue black as that mass of hydrogen we call the sun sinks below the green sea. It will come back tomorrow after a period we call time. I can sit here and repeat the same as I did today, but it will be slightly different because I will be a different person tomorrow and next year and the world a different place a billion years from now. Miracles may be able to last forever.

For me, part of the draw of the seashore is the wind coming off the waves. I have been hypnotized by the shoreline of the Sonoma and Mendocino coasts of California as well as the Oregon coast of haystack rocks and the Washington coast of the Olympic Peninsula. Other than the Maine coast, which I have never seen, I cannot think of any other North American coastline, with the magnificent exception of Alaska, which like everything else is in a class of its own, that would draw me into my philosophical wanderings. These coastlines document the classic meeting of ocean and shore in a worthy struggle for dominance. The sandy beaches of the Gulf and Florida share no epic struggle. The fight is over. The ocean won and the coast gave in. But the cliffs and rock coasts I favor are still in a constant struggle. And the winds that swirl and bounce upwards and outwards with the surf support the battle.

The winds coming out of the fog and mist that define the shore lift the sea gulls and let them soar in a magnificent ballet. The coasts without the birds would be a place not worthy of visiting. The coasts without the cliffs and rocks, offshore and on, take the defiance away from the accompanying winds. The smells of the sea—the salt tang, the dead kelp and seaweed, the fish—all put meaning to the sights and the music of sounds. And if it was possible to tire of the relentless pounding of the waves and cry of the gulls, all you need to do is walk inland to lose your soul to the redwoods, the coastal pine, the grasses and inland dunes that provide the welcome to the land that stopped the sea.

But is it timeless? Hasn't it been here forever? That mystery called time has not allowed that to happen. Time has changed the sea as it has the seashore and the deserts and mountains far inland. Time moves, as do the continents and the mountains. Time has created oceans and it has plowed them under as a peasant plows his field, turning the soil and creating new life. Time flows as relentlessly as do the waves turning rock into sand.

In that desert far inland from the present sea, near where I call home, the rocks used to be the sea floor. The sands were carried by rivers long turned into clouds, which then emptied into seas that covered the continent. No one then stood on the sandy seashore and marveled at the distant blue green horizon. At that time, there was no one, nor was there any other living creature, furred, feathered, or scaled. The seas and coasts have been here forever, but changing with time. Rocks that now sit high atop mountains, a continent away from sea water, used to define oceans. Oceans pounded rocky headlands of seashores now gone forever, torn down and rebuilt a dozen times as water and ice and wind have played their symphony to only themselves.

I listen to waves roll in and roll out, knowing not much will change in my lifetime. I take it on faith that the ocean was not always here and will not always be there. That faith is based on science—geology, chemistry, cosmology, meteorology, evolution of living things. Some people base their faith on something more personal, such as someone who once walked on water. They consider that a miracle. Maybe it is, but to me the overpowering miracle is that the ocean that covered the Colorado Plateau and the Great

Plains disappeared. Fields of lava turned to sand and the sand turned back to stone. Forests that later turned to coal covered the lowlands, and rivers led to that sea. And a diminutive dinosaur evolved feathers and over eons turned into a bald eagle. Miracles come in different forms. Time and what it does is a miracle for me, no more and no less than the miracles of other people.

Philosophers more learned than I have sat on coastlines and pondered larger meanings of what we humans think about and why we act as we do. I cannot compete with them. However, I can do what they cannot. I realize I am unique and I put my life history into focus and determine how I relate to time. We are all different and we all see different things in a wave or a sea lion basking on a rock. Those thoughts become as timeless and infinite as the waves. And as miraculous.

I realized I didn't have to travel to the coast to see the ocean and the miracle of the seashore. I could look out my window in Western Colorado and visualize the vast sea that covered half of Utah and Colorado. A sea that left mud later turned to shale hundreds, even thousands of feet thick at the bottom of that once storm tossed ocean. From my vantage point where I now see mountains and desert, I can sense the presence of that ocean. Its surf beat on a seashore no longer alive with waves that lapped on sandy beaches and floodplains that hid dinosaurs. There were probably no sea gulls and certainly no sea lions, but flying pterosaurs and other reptile ancestors to what I see today may have soared above the waves. Did they call to one another as sea gulls do today? I cannot stand on a beach and look out across this ocean, but in my imagination, I can see that horizon to the east that disappeared beyond the midcontinent seaway, that once stretched from the current Canada to Mexico. The fact I can imagine that distance of time is to me a miracle that competes with the distance across the sea to some unknown land. Given enough time, that sea and that land will disappear, to be replaced by a new sea and a fresh coast of broken cliffs and sandy beaches. Every one, a miracle of time.

Interlude: Time Machine

If we could build one,
When would we go?
Time machines have intrigued us
Since time began.

Why are we not content
With when we know?
We are never content
With what we know.

We can change the what's and who's
But not the when's.
That is given, with no chance for change.
We are drawn to the difficult.

Give me the past.
I lived it and left it behind.
Or it left me behind
Before I arrived.

The future unknown is for others.
They wish to know how things turn out.
I might be amused,
But also upset that I didn't change what was to be.

I think I am given one chance
To be me; this may be true.
But I may be more than me.
Forward or backward I might reappear.

Not as me, not as you,
But another soul.
In another time
And another world.

This adds a new dimension
To the idea of a parallel world.
I would be busy looking for the wormhole
To connect the two.

If my time machine worked,
Could I turn it off and stop to visit?
What if I landed underwater
Or on the top of a volcano?

Could I circle and hover,
Deciding whether to land and explore?
Too many questions with no answers.
Would I get a second chance?

INTERLUDE: SANTA FE NIGHT

The night over Santa Fe blurs the nearby hills.
Wind rustles the aspen leaves,
Chased by the spirits of old.
Life has happened here for a long time.
Longer than coyote, longer than owl.

The clouds pass overhead
On silent journey.
Seeing what they always have seen,
But now manmade flash and glitter
Obliterates even the moon.

Pueblos replaced by padres
Traders replaced by builders.
Now Hummers and New Age crystals
Drown out even the chants and rattles
That echo from the silence of old.

Magic still hides in the breeze.
Spirits that hold onto lizard tails,
Onto hummingbird wings
That flit and dart rock to rock, flower to flower,
Quietly disappear.

Listen to the silence,
Watch the moon fade on the horizon.
Embrace it before the sun melts the dew,
And wilts the primrose,
Making way for new blooms tonight.

History in Time

But what has been will be —
First memory, then oblivion's swallowing sea;
Like men foregone, shall we merge into those
Whose story no one knows.

Thomas Hardy, "The To-be-forgotten,"
Poems of the Past and Present

———◆———

In rivers the water that you touch
Is the last of what has passed,
And the first of that which comes.
So with time present.

Leonardo da Vinci,
Notebooks of Leonardo da Vinci

THE QUARRY

I stood at the quarry looking to the west. The wide canyon of Escalante Creek stretched below me; the inconspicuous mass of the Uncompahgre Plateau was the western horizon. Katherine and I were being escorted along a trail to the Dry Mesa Quarry, given lots of interesting information on dinosaurs and red rocks and university research. This was the largest dinosaur quarry in the world. *Really? It seemed so small for that.* It had hidden rare and huge dinosaurs. *How can they tell that from such small fragments of skeletons?* This was a logjam of assorted bones that identified some Jurassic creek bed. *OK.*

Once a year, Brigham Young University, the special-use permittee who operated the quarry, in conjunction with the Forest Service, manager of the land, had an open house for the public to view this jewel of dinosaurian research. As with most such endeavors, it was isolated, in the middle of trackless nowhere. Of course, that's where you find such things. You don't find them in downtown Denver. As with gold and jewels, you find them where they are, not where you'd like them to be for convenience.

An hour and a half from Delta, Colorado, the quarry was perched on the edge of the Uncompahgre Plateau,

overlooking miles of red rock and piñon forest. It had
survived millennia of eagles soaring overhead and lizards
skulking about underfoot, thunderstorms in August and
blowing snow in December. And the bones just lay there
hidden for eons, ready to guard their secrets forever until
the next big bang started the cycle over again.

I listened to the geologic story, one that I was familiar
with. We were on the Morrison Formation, a collection
of muds and sands and the decay of millions of years of
interesting life from a long, long time ago. In other places,
the Morrison was still buried by thousands of feet of other
types of rock. Here, this was ground level. The Morrison
met the sky. Above us lay not the Dakota Sandstone, nor
the Mancos Shale, nor the rubble of basalt. Just blue sky
and time, however you could see it or measure it. But it
lay heavy on me, blowing with the zephyr of a west wind
and taunting me with secrets I could never know. These
missing overlying formations used to hide the Morrison.
Where did they go?

Below in the canyon lay the Kayenta, the Wingate,
and the usual litany of western sediment. They contained
no fossils, no evidence of the world they were part of. But
here, in the Morrison, the conditions met under a Jurassic
sky, below the Mesozoic equivalent of the yet to occur
Little Dipper and Orion's belt, on a sphere called Earth, and
bones were preserved. Creatures we will never know lived
and died and were buried in mud, then covered as they
sank deeper and deeper into Mother Earth. They rested,
then they turned to stone by countless millennia of seeping
water and silica chemistry. Slowly they were jostled and
vibrated as the earth moved around them. Once upon a
time at sea level, they now rest thousands of feet closer to
an Orion that slowly appeared in a changing sky. They,

and the Wingate and Kayenta and the others pushed
upward. Sort of an honorable thing to happen, I thought.
They became the Plateau. They replaced something that
once gave itself to create them. This once again brought
up the whole subject of Colorado Plateau geology that
never failed to transform my consciousness. I won't get
into that here. Just suffice it to say, time passed, rocks
became sand, sand became rock, rock rolled down the
rivers as red sand once again.

And caught in this symphony of time were dinosaurs,
one small event in the millions of years we witnessed from
this quarry. Think about what we spend so much time and
money on—a few bones. But these are bones of dinosaurs.
Something that was the essence of life on earth for longer
than we can ever hope to envision, something that no
longer exists. We see no allosaurs stalking their prey today,
we hear no trumpets of stegosaurs like we hear elk bugle
in the September aspen. We hear no thundering vibration
of earth as the supersaurus, or was it the ultrasaurus,
wanders by, eating whole trees in its quest to stay alive
day to day.

What is our fascination with these creatures? Is it
because they no longer exist? We really have no idea
what they looked like. With all the fuss over T. rex, do
we realize there are fewer than a dozen specimens of
this monster that have ever been found? We don't know
what its skin looked like, what its eyes saw, what sounds
it made. Modern science can do wonders with little bits
of information like a toe bone or tooth. But can it create
the living, breathing thing that laid the eggs and then
came back to care for the young? Did this thing called the
allosaur stalk its prey with the cunning of the coyote? Did
it look up in the sky to watch the meteors and northern

lights? Did it mate for life like a Canada goose, or just come
together for a few seconds to mate like the elk that now
walks over the graves of the bones?

Our kids are fascinated by dinosaurs. We conjure
up such images and mystique over these animals. I
theorize that it is a safe thing to do. Imagine in a place
like Western Colorado idolizing the wolf or grizzly.
That is just not politically correct or uncontroversial.
Idolizing the allosaurs and T. rexes doesn't necessitate
preserving their habitat, which in turn raises unsolvable
controversies involving cattlemen and loggers and states'
rights advocates. Or the religious right or Save the Allosaur
Society, and countless other groups calling for one side or
another. No, it's safe with dinosaurs. There are none left, so
we can wow at their size, and marvel at the skeletons we
put together from a few bones gathered at a site like this.
It's safe to invent and theorize what they were like and
where they lived and what they ate. They didn't interfere
with us; they had no Dinosaur Unlimited clubs looking
after them. They just waded in the swamps and wandered
the streams minding their own business, for millions of
years, no less. I wonder if Homo sapiens will last even one
million before destroying himself and half the life on this
earth with him.

Our group stood by the quarry watching the
volunteers pick with screwdrivers and brush away sand
with paintbrushes. So delicately they worked, exposing
something that had lain hidden for millions upon millions
of years. Lying there in sunlight for the first time in eons
was a large bone—a shoulder bone according to the
museum curator. And over there was a jumble of foot and
toe bones of an allosaur. We make so much of bones. They
are not even the real bones. They are replicas of the real

bone, carbon replaced by silica. They are cracked and fragile. But they indicate the real thing.

Can we really appreciate what we are seeing? This fossilized bone is something that was of this earth, but lived in a world that no longer exists. Her world was something we cannot even comprehend. The land was not the same, the plants no longer exist, the air was different. We would be as lost in her world as she would be in ours. Jurassic Park movies to the contrary, she shared the space we now call home, but we could never co-exist. She lived in a time so remote, we have as little comprehension of it as she would of reading a computer program of ours. But she lived here. She walked this very area, mated, raised her young. She hunted for food and died a lonely death right here within sight of where we all stood. But we don't and cannot share that life. What to me now is a forest of pine and juniper, with sandstone underfoot, was in this very spot once before, a swamp or riverbed carrying sand from towering mountains that no longer exist and haven't for more time than I can even count.

We should cover this quarry with a roof and make a statue of the allosaur on the front wall, put in a huge stained glass window that overlooks Escalante Creek and hold religious service here every Sunday, or Monday, or whatever day we consider sacred. We should sing hymns to this spot and pray to the spirits of these beasts that ruled here. We should get on our knees and kiss the sandstone and say a hail rex or two to the sky. We should lay our hand on a piece of Wingate sandstone and think about the time that has passed since this rock was nothing but sand howling across a barren desert under a blue gray sky, free of nitrous oxides and ozone pollution. What god ruled this life, long before we jostled among ourselves and competed with Buddha, Mohammed, Isis, or Jesus?

Too many of us have lost the reverence for the life around us, living as well as stone. This was just one small piece of earth that was revealing its secrets. But those secrets hidden a week short of forever, give us a small glimpse of something that should humble us all. The time that has passed in unending insignificance since the life that once was here, has evolved into the life that stands here now as reverent as any god we worship now.

Did any of the dozen people in our little tour group understand what we were witnessing? Or were we lost on the images of those plastic toy dinosaurs that roar and bellow when we insert the batteries? We fantasize on the teeth of the T. rex and the small size of the brain of the ultrasaur. Then we drive away from the lonely site on Dry Mesa and return to our lives today. Millions of years from now, who will stand here and marvel at the fossilized bones of researchers and their rusted screwdrivers and clipboards? I turned away from the quarry and walked up the road to my car. I listened for some distant bellow and roar. I heard only a lone chickadee sing into the endless wind.

ANOTHER DAY IN PARADISE

Another day in paradise, I thought, as I walked down the sandy road while a warm October sun was slowly breaking the chill of the early morning air. Miles onto the plateau, nearing Harts Point south of Moab, we parked on a rocky flat where unbroken slickrock erased the path of the road. Choosing to walk, we wandered through the cryptobiotic soil, carefully hopping from rock to rock to avoid breaking the life-giving crust. Maybe not my perfect ideal of paradise, but a calming experience in a soul-enlightening piece of earth. It certainly was close enough to call paradise, beating any other feasible alternative at that time.

The canyon to the west played hide and seek through the piñon and juniper branches. We could see the salmon orange Wingate wall below us, snaking along the side canyon that led out to the lower expanse of Harts Basin and the hidden Colorado River. Above it lay the smooth sandstone of a formation whose name I chose not to try and remember. I used to know the names of all these formations, but I since decided names hid the details and numbed the senses as well as the imagination. But the Wingate—that you do not forget. It stands formidable throughout the Colorado Plateau, like the very idea of the expanse of time it broods over.

We walked over an outcrop of nearly flat slickrock, but with scattered shallow potholes that reminded me what the Canadian Shield may have looked like from 30,000 feet above the earth soon after the glacier melted. Nearly level, with flat bottomed depressions, the lichen dotted sandstone gently undulated over several acres. The rain of two days ago left many depressions with an inch of water. Some were larger, with mud filled bottoms. I envisioned these as the ancestral Great Lakes of my imaginary Canada. Some of the higher knolls had plate-sized circular rims, like a melted down sandcastle.

At the edge of the bedrock outcrop, where sand and soil took over once again, we found the flakes. Small chips of flint or chert, smooth yet jagged-edged rock, dotted the ground. I imagined this was where someone sat hundreds, even thousands of years before, patiently chipping larger rocks into tools. It could have been. Few people ever came this way anymore, and those who did, as evidenced by the tire tracks, were more intent on churning up the fragile soil than in getting out and walking to see what they might find. This hidden spot could possibly have lain undisturbed for centuries. I preferred to think it was as I unleashed my imagination.

I thought back to that earlier time. Was it just another day in paradise for that person who sat or squatted here? Did he think of living in paradise? How could he even imagine such a concept? This, and the area within a hundred mile radius, was the only world he knew. He never realized there was an Alaskan wilderness, a Mississippi River, a Mendocino coast. He didn't know what retirement was, or a vacation, or the faintest hint of the time span the rocks below him encompassed. This was home and it was all that was. Every day was a day in paradise, or more likely another day to survive.

Not a Monday or Thursday or Fourth of July. One more day, sunshine or rain, he sat here chipping flint to make points and scrapers. He had a name, a family, a responsibility. I ached to talk to him, to ask him questions that flooded my mind as I looked at the ground he sat on and at the discards of his skillful work. How many sunsets, how many lightning flashes that shot through the hot summer sky as he thought of the deer, the bighorn, even the rabbits his points would kill? His food supply depended on the effectiveness of his tools. The chips, they were of no value. Reddish brown, white, flecked pink and lavender— just garbage left over. It was the excess that hid the true shape he was searching for, just like a perfect Carrera marble sculpture by Michelangelo.

I bent over and picked up several chips, inspecting them, feeling the smooth sides, the jagged edges. These were not just flakes, some archaeological reject. They were what was left as some hunter of another world, another age, sat here one day. Or many. A real person, a son, a husband, a father. He could tell me so much that I didn't know, so much that neither I nor anyone else could ever know. He played as a child, followed his father on hunts, learned the skills, climbed down the cliffs as winter covered this high plateau with cold and snow, lived along what we now call Indian Creek far below until the summer sun drew him and his clan back up onto the cooler plateau where game was more plentiful. I will never know his name, nor will I ever know the secrets he could tell. I and my kind are so much poorer for that.

What did he think as he skillfully and patiently tapped one rock on another? Was he teaching his son, maybe his nephew in his matrilineal society? Did he ask the blessing of his gods to sharpen his skill? His camp had to be nearby. Unlike me, he did not drive 40 miles to visit here, to stand in awe of the cliffs below. This was a person who was routinely earning his living, using a skill that meant life or death to him and those who depended on him.

Did he marvel at the canyons below? Did he walk
in amazement over the geologic formation that I saw as
a miniature Canada from the air, before soil and forest
covered most of the rock? I doubt it. That was beyond his
comprehension. He was a simple man, uncomplicated by
pondering questions he didn't even know to ask. He and
his people lived a routine life, the same as hundreds of
generations before him. He sat here one day, or several,
chipping his rocks, creating works of art that were nothing
other than his means of staying alive. I marvel at the
precision and skill he must have had. He had the patience
I could never have in this hectic world I live in. Maybe he
considered his world hectic as well, struggling every day,
never able to think ahead to a simple life of relaxation.

His world is gone to me, just as tons of rock that lined
his cliffs are gone as well. Gone as gravity and rainfall
slowly eroded an inch here, a foot there. Time was only
a concept that he understood as one day turning into
another. Time that I understand as more sunrises and
sunsets than he could count in his lifetime and the lifetime
of all his ancestors.

I cradled a handful of red and white chips. A chickadee
broke my time travel as he called his impatient song
from a nearby juniper. That small impertinent bird was
doing what his ancestors had done for even longer than
my chipmaker. That very bird could trace his ancestors
thousands upon thousands of years back, to this very spot.
Like my chipmaker, he knew no other life. His ancestor
called that very song to this unknown man, who listened
to the constant scolding one October day long, long ago.

I talked to the chickadee, as I did to the spirit of that
long forgotten man. He created these chips with his own

hands. I held his spirit and begged to know for one minute
the world he saw as he sat here. Maybe now, he speaks to
me through the little bird. I asked him to let me take a few
of his discards. He shouldn't care. He will live on now, in
a world he could not imagine. I try and imagine his as I
cradle the flakes in my hand. I will gather what patience I
have to wait for the chips to talk to me, the only remaining
clues from a world gone forever.

THE TRESTLE

I stood by the trestle one evening and watched the sun set over the northern wall of the Sierra. Nestled on the edge of the valley and protected from discovery by the forest of pine and fir and cedar, this artifact of railroad logging at the turn of the century was off the well-traveled roads, neglected and forgotten for decades.

I discovered this trestle on one of my wanderings the other day. It was a pleasant surprise—a neglected old railroad trestle standing as a silent reminder of an abandoned railroad grade built by logging companies in a hopeful time long ago. It represented a way of life lost to a time unfamiliar to me. The rotting logs were moss-covered gray skeletons with a strength weakened by the snows and winds of a century of winters. I stood underneath, looking up at the heights, peering through the vigorous trunks of a new generation of fir and cedar. They nearly reached to the top of the trestle.

Laboriously climbing up the rocky slope, I stood at the top, on the trace of the old railroad grade, looking across the missing bridge. The trestle itself was mostly intact, but not its top. I looked behind me to see how this missing piece fit in. Along the old grade, only an occasional tie was left to mark the line, now covered by sagebrush, rock, and dirt. A former scar, it was gently healing with time and gravity. The missing bridge made no difference. But what was missing? I listened to see if I could hear a story from the past.

I closed my eyes and listened through the stillness,

past the bird twitters, past the ageless breeze through
the tree tops. I could hear the steady approaching cough
of the locomotive. I could see the puff of steam clouds. I
could hear the loneliest sound of all—the mournful wail
of the locomotive whistle. I felt the creak of the new wood
held by massive pins of iron. I even heard the laugh of the
engineer, or was it the fireman, tossing chunks of pine into
the firebox.

I heard the whack of a two-bitted axe into the tall pines
standing majestically on the ridge top and the crash as
they fell to earth. The neighing of the work horses echoed
over the massive trees now lying prone on the ground.
The clink and rattle of the chains wrapped around the
logs added a feeling of power and strength. The horses
struggled to pull the logs across the red dirt. Needles and
branches, the detritus of the once proud trees, were left to
cover the ground as remains of what once was an ancient
forest. The pines, serving as food and homes for countless
generations of squirrels, porcupines, and birds, would
serve to build houses and stores for a growing generation
of pioneers down in Reno and Sacramento. The trainload
of naked logs slowly left the remaining forest, watched by
the curious deer as if it was a funeral procession heading
to the cemetery. In a way, it was.

The pounding of iron, the hissing of steam, the clank
of an empty can of pipe tobacco tossed over the hill—
these were sharp in my mind's ear. I smiled as I thought
of the denuded hillside of a century ago, now reclaimed
as a new forest, full of hope and energy, reminding me of
the recuperative power of that force we call nature. Our
world is patient and forgiving and apathetic to me and my
kind. We can build narrow gauge railroads into a former
wilderness, we can fell the mighty giants, gouge the earth

as we take what isn't ours to take, and then we can step
back and wait a century or two. The power we create and
display can be eroded into a faint memory by a few seeds
and squirrels.

As I imagined the growth and renewal, I noticed the
stillness. I could almost hear the pine cones form, open
to release their seeds, then gently fall to the receiving
earth. I opened my eyes and heard the coyote cry out the
history lesson to her descendants. In the early days, the
men came, and the wood and steel snake rolled along lines
of iron. They cut the trees and dug trails in the earth. The
railroad left, but the men who cut the trees did not.

The sun set tonight as it has for a million eagles over
centuries, soaring across the red evening sky. A time of
peace and a time of man, but peace is here again—or still.
Men came and left their mark but they did not destroy.
They do not take what cannot be taken. They borrowed—a
few trees, a little dirt, some silence. And they left a few
pounds of rusting iron nails, slowly returning to the soil as
surely as the sun sets every evening.

I came into this theater late. The play was over and
the hall empty. But I heard the echoes of the shouts and
laughter. The props were left and the dreams were laid
down on the floor for me to pick up and polish to life.
I missed this drama, but I'll play it in my mind, hidden
amidst the twitter of birds and the ageless breeze through
the pine tops and the coyote tracks in the dirt washed
down on the grade. Even that will soon be gone, from both
me and the rain.

Aging Campgrounds

The twilight was fading into a shadowy darkness, dulling the red soil and red rocks. The lights of Fruita glowed far below like a land-based Milky Way. We walked through the campground's Loop C, closed according to the sign on the cable barriers.

Loop C was surely the original campground up here on top of Colorado National Monument. Was it closed for the season, now well into October and past the bewitching hour for summer tourists? Or has it been closed permanently, past its prime, past its usefulness?

I felt the loss of something significant as we wound our way along the cracked asphalt path from the parking lot to the amphitheater. I was walking through history, a time now leaving us as too many sunsets have cast their red glow over the twisted juniper and eroded sandstone bedrock. Recent rains left their mark as gullies and washes flowing downhill, leaving red sand deposited across the path and road in patterns similar to those now fossilized in the sandstone bedrock all around us. Eroded gullies crisscrossed the area, like wrinkles on the face of an aging movie star.

I winced as I walked, realizing this whole area, and what it once meant, was like that same aging beauty queen, admired in her day for her unblemished beauty. Those sunsets had taken their toll in time indeed. What forty years ago was a fine campground, with new tables, an asphalt road, state-of-the-art amphitheater, and restroom, was now a dilapidated artifact. People once came up here to listen to the Ranger talk, to pitch their tent, to smell the piñon fragrance, and hear the wind fall off the Wingate cliffs to the oven baked valley below. The times were simpler then, people's patience longer, and expectations lower. The National Parks and Monuments held a reverence; we learned why from our parents.

I realized things weren't the same anymore. A beleaguered bureaucracy now was forced to cut, trim, eliminate, modify with a staff that didn't share that same reverence, that awe that I had. It was a job like any other with too much political interference. I represented the changes myself. Whereas forty years ago, I would have been thrilled to pitch a new tent in a flat spot under a twisted juniper, now I sat in a campsite parked with my new travel trailer in Loop B, the newer part of the campground with level pull-through units, next to the flush toilets with laser operated faucets and electricity. My years in the Forest Service bureaucracy had jaded me into a cynicism for all the pampered campers who didn't stop to smell the juniper fire (which now was not allowed here) or listen to the scrub jays (not that you could hear anything over the muted roar of the electric generator of every RV).

We left the old asphalt path, with the hand-cemented sandstone slabs as curbs, and moved onto the old campground road with its short spurs (no pull-throughs here) and rotted log cribs marking the once flat tent pads. The sign posts with campsite numbers were tilted and uprooted, giving one more indication of neglect. More wrinkles on the beautiful face of the aging work of art. Time passes, people change. We see it in the gutted downtowns of small towns across the country. We see it in the small campgrounds across the West, now abandoned and put to bed. The old campgrounds of the parks are now revamped to fit the big RVs, the demands for all the conveniences never even dreamed of forty years ago.

I felt like Rip Van Winkle, blinking like an owl, wondering what happened. Did I sleep through forty years? I looked up at the steadily darkening sky, no sunset red left in the scattered clouds, stars turning on like the electric lights in the new toilet building. I listened to the crickets, unchanged in their forty generations, as they ended their arias before frost ended them for the year. I rubbed my face, feeling my own wrinkles. Yes, the beauty of this old campground was still here, as is the beauty in the old movie star's face. But we tend to ignore our own wrinkles and remember the way we were once before.

We change, as does the land. The rocks slowly erode sand grain by sand grain. Even the oldest gnarled juniper dies eventually, but not before a new generation lifts branches up and above the shrinking height of the twisted patriarch. Chipmunks live and die as do the chickadees flitting from tree to tree. As do we. The world is for the young, most often ignoring the wisdom of the old. Wrinkles don't mean senility; a gnarled old juniper with half dead branches doesn't mean decay. For me, I see an increased power and beauty—wisdom if you will—in a patriarchal old tree. But we tend to put a fence around these ancient ones and marvel at their resilience and thin hold on life. We forget that tree was young and vibrant. So too with ourselves and these things we held dear in our vibrant youth.

We left Loop C and walked the nearly dark road to the comfort of our trailer and its electric lights and comfy beds. I looked in the mirror and yes, there were wrinkles and gray hair. But I remembered the time when Loop C would have been new and modern. I was new and

innocent then too. I watched all those sunsets over the
years and I listened to the ravens soaring overhead and felt
the breeze on my face. Now, as the sand grains continued
their slow, slow journey down the mountain to the river and
then the sea, I realized my journey had a long way to go as
well. I had as much to look forward as I could see behind.
Some things change, some things die. But the sun keeps
setting and the wind still carries the call of the chickadee.
You just have to listen for it. It will always be there.

OF BRAMBLES
AND OLD FENCES

I had been cooped up for too many cloudy, cool, and snowy winter days in my new home on a piece of property and time once belonging to a lonely hermit lady. On a January day, I stood outside, breathing in the warmth of the intense blue sky, trying to decide what to do next in my cleanup of the property. There was so much I had to do to erase that earlier time and make way for my own time. I had brush to uproot, tin cans to dig out of the frozen soil, trails to maintain, the cabin to clean out.

The cabin. That was a multiyear project, but it beckoned me. The cabin was the magnet that pulled at me from years gone by. It was Hazel and Walt, the old homesteaders. It was the remains of their life. There was not much else left of them. There were a few old car parts that Walt had drug onto the place and scavenged for something usable, something worth a dollar. Old stoves and barrels and buckets and rusted junk still dotted the hillside. Everything he thought was worth anything, he brought here. And it still lay scattered amongst the sagebrush and juniper, rusting and rotting. The pack rats filled the cabin and surrounded me with their distinctive repulsive and disgusting smell.

Now, the cabin where Walt and Hazel spent long January nights huddled by the wood stove was one giant rat nest. Since it was hard to even get to the cabin, hidden and protected by brambles, I decided to start cleaning up the yard, or what was left of a yard. It was now filled with an obnoxious thorny purple-flowered bush that had taken over the yard and surrounding hillside. The other brambles intermixed with this bush were yellow roses, long gone wild and unruly. I was leaving them for now, but at least cleaning them of dead branches, already aged enough to be sporting colorful lichens on their weathered stems.

Maybe at one time, Hazel had planted the obnoxious thorny purple-flowered bush as a hedge or maybe it just appeared. However it got here, and whatever it was, it had gone wild, taking over with its expanding root system and penetrating thorns. I dug and pulled and uprooted off and on for several years. It only seemed to be invigorated by this jostling of its roots. It came up again in force, but smaller. Maybe by attrition, I could wear it down. That is, if I didn't wear down my fingers and legs from the thorns. It was tough on gloves. The thorns always seemed to find the holes in my gloves. And my gloves always seemed to have holes, no matter how new they were. But this was a war and I was determined to win. Until I did, the going was tough.

The problem with the yard was that the bushes had grown up and around and into old chicken wire and woven wire fences that used to delineate something. They may have kept in or out, the chickens or pigs or goats or other menagerie that kept Hazel and Walt in some type of food. The fences were only kept standing now by the brush, and in order to take out one, I had to take out both. Anyone who has ever had to pull out morning glory or other spreading vine from a fence can understand this struggle. But it was a magnitude or two worse with these bushes since they not only had thorns, they grew over the years up to ten feet tall and with a woody stem two or three inches in diameter. Even if I uprooted them, which I had to do, then I could spend hours slowly weaving the branches out from the wire. I came to hate chicken wire. In a way, I admired these ancient plants since most of the older stems were covered with lichens and moss. Beauty covered ugliness and despair.

I had to stop and actually chuckle on occasion, thinking of Hazel so proudly assembling her fences out of whatever scraps of barbed wire, wood, posts, sheep fencing, and baling wire she had on hand (probably from Walt's collection of wire and scrap lumber). She built a fence, and no doubt it worked for whatever purpose she had in mind. But now the half-buried rotting bottom boards, wired onto the rusted and mangled chicken wire fence, held together by these cursed branches, somehow had an obstinacy that I had to respect. They brought to life the stubbornness of Hazel that I could only imagine as she cheerfully whistled while she wired the fence together on some forgotten October afternoon long ago.

As I was taking a break from my uprooting and cursing, I stood by the front of the cabin. My pulling of brush had revealed details of a front window that had been hidden by the tangled mass of dead branches. This window was not your normal window, but two old Model something or other vintage car or truck windows, held in place by bent nails. Most of the windows in the cabin had long fallen out, with broken glass lying on the ground and window frames hanging in various stages of rot or disarray. This was Hazel and maybe Walt at their best. They had used some of Walt's cars as a source, quite ingenious actually, for a window.

How long had this treasure of a window lain hidden in the southeast corner wall of the porch? Twenty years?

Thirty? Probably more since Hazel had been dead for ten years. And Walt for over forty. I thought back to when this innovation was new. Did Walt install it, or did Hazel make do in those thirty years she hermitted this place by herself? I know she had to be a resourceful old gal. The walls of the cabin were papered with old newspapers held into place with canning jar lids nailed on the wall. This in itself had amazed me when I first inspected this cabin after we bought the property. I was struck by the "Vote for Ike and Dick" full-page newspaper ad of 1952. Walt was alive then. Did Walt and Hazel chuckle as they papered the dining room with this bit of democratic pride? Somehow I doubt that they represented the intellectual elite of voting society, but it was possible they sat around the cabin at night discussing the qualities of Eisenhower versus Stevenson after enjoying a supper of home canned potatoes, pork chops, and apricot pie, all raised from their own garden and home butchering. Maybe these rusted fences I had been earnestly tearing down kept the pig safe from pillaging coyotes and mountain lions. Then again, maybe not.

After my discovery of the car-window window, I found myself just standing there talking to the cabin. What did go on at one time long ago in this dilapidated ruin of a house? Hazel lived here for such a long time after Walt fell over dead in 1958. He had a varied and interesting life, was a jack of all trades and obviously a scrounger. But because he left so long ago, I didn't think of him very often. I thought of Hazel. I could look in the cabin and visualize her sitting alone by the wood stove. I saw her watching TV, however limited or poor her reception probably was. I saw her tending her cats and living with her memories. She rarely left the property and became more and more reclusive.

This cabin and immediate surroundings were her life. This view, like some grand and epic Moran painting of distant mountains and multicolored sunset clouds, was her world.

I looked inside at the mess. There were rags and old beaten down cardboard boxes littering the floor. The newspaper wallpaper was in tatters. The roof leaked, but this didn't matter since the windows were mostly gone. There were two refrigerators, covered with streaked rat and who knows what else droppings. This remnant of a person's life was in total disarray and filth. In her prime, would Hazel have been bothered by what had happened to her home? I had no idea. The pioneers had dirt floors, but that didn't make them dirty. A newspaper wall covering may have seemed bothersome to me, but it served its purpose and certainly could be more interesting than the most expensive brocaded French wallpaper.

I could have rambled on in my mind as I stared into the front porch with its old mattress and rusting bedsprings. As in any old building, what is left in tattered ruins by the passage of time could only hint at the former inhabitants. The pack rats and weasels, ground squirrels and mice now called this home. No telephone to interrupt the February night's silence; no glare of TV with Lawrence Welk dancing amid the champagne bubbles.

That loneliness of a former life kept invading my thoughts as I dug and yanked at the bushes now creeping up through the logs and boards of the front porch walls. I tore the rolled asphalt siding off the old boards, exposing the brown and orange weathering of old wood planks. Some of the long exposed boards were now brightly covered with green and red and orange lichens, matching that on the oldest of the bushes. I crunched rusted old tin cans as I walked. They, and old light bulbs, bottles, and assorted other garbage, were half buried in the yard. Time was covering the old blight left by a lonely old lady. Time was eating away at the cabin, but my impatience would not allow it to continue at such a slow pace much longer. Steadily, but more quickly than the natural process, I was removing the story of this old lady and her long dead companion.

Trying to continue with my work and not think of the history of the place, I uncovered an old pitchfork, lying entangled in vines and grass. I thought of the last time it was used. The handle was almost rotted off, but was somehow held together by colorful lichens. As I dug into the rock border next to the porch, which once held iris or daisy or other colorful flowerbeds, I uncovered an old pick. It was almost entirely buried and the handle held onto the rusted metal by only a fiber. Then an old hoe. Ducking from a sudden darkness, I gazed overhead as an eagle soared across the sun, casting a menacing but awe inspiring shadow across the entire cabin. I thought about a similar eagle flying over here nearly a half century ago as Walt laid this pick against the side of the house. He had been digging in the back yard, working on the old cistern. The ground was unmercifully rocky and he needed the pick. He laid it aside as he stopped for an afternoon lemonade and may never have touched it again. Hazel had probably used the hoe to hack weeds out of her potatoes and beans. She may also have used the pitchfork to throw hay to the old milk cow. It was set against the fence and remained there after the old cow died and Hazel could never again afford to buy a new source of milk. The pitchfork sat there until a strong storm one May afternoon blew it over, never to see the sun again until this January afternoon.

What story did the old gutter have, now swinging in the wind, hanging by only a thin strand of rusted bailing wire? The old stock tank rusted through, lying next to the row of crumbling truck tires. The pieces of still white painted sheets of an old metal shed, buried in the cheatgrass. The two squares of rusted wire window screen, crumpled underneath the pile of bottles.

In my mind, I could hear the scuffle of the pigs and cackle of the long gone chickens. I listened for the laughter or even the sighs of an old lady who had locked out the rest of the world. Her world would be here until all traces of her vanished. Someday the cabin would be gone, replaced by fruit trees or berry bushes, or something productive for me. I would put my mark on this former homestead, then leave it for another soul some day long in the future to contemplate who I was.

I had spent the day in the front yard. There was still a day's work left there, just clearing it enough to be able to walk through. I left the rose bushes untouched, save the clearing of dead branches. I left the side yard and back for another day, another week, another year. There was still the old root cellar, earth roof caving in, log beams cracking and sagging onto the rows of jars and bottles. There was still the unknown mess lying next to the side room, hiding who knows what? And of course there was the inside of the cabin, waiting for a good mask to protect me from unknown and dangerous microbes and viruses and other poisons from the layers of filth. That was all to wait until a later day.

Shaking my head as I felt the past tugging at me, I knew I could not escape the images of an earlier time. I understood it and I appreciated it. But, like Hazel and even Walt, I realized I was temporary as well. Once I or anyone

else leaves a place, nature calmly and patiently takes over
and undoes everything we tried to do. At some future time,
the cabin would be gone, as would be the memories of
Hazel. I wanted to learn her life and capture her memories.
I slowly peeled away memories as I uprooted bushes and
tore down boards. The flames and smoke from the pile
of boards and brush would eventually send all memories
floating on the west wind. Then there would be simply
the chattering of the titmice and the fleeting shadow of
the eagle, riding the wind of his kingdom. There would
be only the sound of the wind as the clouds floated by on
some sunny January afternoon far in the future. Then,
eventually, there would be no memories.

BYRON'S FLOWER

The old book called to me. It deserved a better fate than sitting on the shelf in the Paonia Library basement for their used book sale. Forgotten, water stained, passed over in a century's worth of shadows of some dusty bookshelf or attic chest. I picked it up carefully, its binding held together by threads. The old cloth cover was warped and faded by age, but the embossed title still held the majesty it once enjoyed. Byron's Poems. I thumbed to the title page, as I always do on old books, looking for the date of printing. It was missing, torn out decades ago. What caught my eye though, was the inside cover. Ancient handwriting from some long dead hand flowed with the style and art of a forgotten age.

Glenwood, Colorado, August 9, '93

I would here pen a poem but it would be too easily compared with the powerful products of the gifted author of this volume. It would be as the firefly in the brilliant sunlight.

Remember me as one who possesses the will, the depths of emotion, the sympathy and love of romance and the beautiful, but, who lacks the power to express.

A Friend

I didn't take the time to carefully read the flowery handwriting until I got home. There I examined my prize of several old books of poetry by Byron, Longfellow,

Browning. To me, when any library discards such works of art, it is both a crime, and a sad ending to a glory unnoticed today. We throw these books away to make room for the works of today's popular writers of murder, mystery, and mediocrity.

I read and reread this handwritten dedication. A friend, afraid to open their heart in poem, penned an even more powerful expression of love for this unknown person. Was it some lovelorn man trying to impress a lady friend? Or a gentle young woman trying to tame her rugged man of the mountains? I will never know, but this makes it all the more powerful to me. Both have long ago gone to their maker, now together reading poetry of love to each other. My mind paints the picture and beautiful it is, full of color and delicate details.

Byron could pen the words and poems of rhyme and rhythm, of love and beauty. But this friend outdid the best of Byron, for his or her words were from the heart and personal, opening their very soul. Did the two sit together, framed by the majesty of the Colorado Rockies, lulled by the flowing water of a mountain stream, hypnotized by the rustling aspen leaves overhead? Or so enamored of each other, reading aloud the love poems of Lord Byron, were they deaf to the outside world?

Was she here in the high mountains of Colorado to escape tuberculosis, like so many at the turn of the century? Or maybe she was a nurse caring for the cowboys and miners, looking for romance or running from a love gone sour back East. Was he working in the mines of Aspen, looking for his fortune, or was he a logger harvesting the trees to build the mines or the fancy homes of the mine owners? My questions exhausted me, especially since I knew I would never find answers.

I thumbed through the book, careful as I turned the brittle pages. The print was tiny, the names of the poems mostly unfamiliar to me, although a few I recognized. Then, as I turned to page 425, I saw the flower. The emotion hit me like a chunk of Colorado granite. Tucked among the pages of the poem called 'The Corsair', and faded to transparency by a century of lost time, was a pressed flower. Color and species now unknowable, but possibly a mountain flower such as a gentian, it lay forgotten since the day the book was laid down for the last time.

What was the story of this flower, this symbol of the love unspoken, or maybe spoken softly in a mountain meadow? Was it the friend and the nameless lover? Or had their love melted as the winter snows, to be replaced by a new friend. The facts will never be known, so I create my own truth to satisfy my hunger for answers.

It was the friend who had given her the book, knowing she loved Byron and the romantic poets. They were reclining in a flower-filled alpine meadow, listening to the gentle twittering of the mountain bluebirds, the whisper of the breeze coming off the high peaks nearby. She was reading Byron to him, his attention only on her innocent beauty. They were in love at the end of the 19th century, oblivious to the world. Their world existed only in each other that sun filled Sunday afternoon. He picked the sky blue gentian and gently put it in her aspen yellow hair. She smiled at him and slowly took it out to mark the page she had been reading. They never returned to the page. The flower stayed there until I opened the book. Did some tragedy tear them apart, never to return to the painful memories evoked by the power of Byron?

Some mysteries remain forever, as ethereal and diaphanous as that August alpine afternoon. Countless stories of love and infatuation are written and unwritten. Some fade away over time as softly as the gentian. Some end in sorrow, some bitterly. But I know, as I read with my own emotion, this love, so full of mystery, will endure forever. It started with a book of Byron's poems and an inscription so full of tenderness and hesitant beauty. This book will endure forever as well, even as it turns to ashes and dust. I may read some of the poems, but I turn the pages gently and with reverence for the love expressed so long ago by someone who will forever remain unknown to me.

I gently moved the flower to read the words underneath, now slightly stained by the flower itself. Surely coincidence that these were the words so marked, I thought, as I read them slowly, hesitantly.

> *But bound and fixed in fettered solitude,*
> *To pine, the prey of every changing mood;*
> *To gaze on thine own heart; and meditate*
> *Irrevocable faults and coming fate—*
> *Too late the last to shun—the first to mend—*
> *To count the hours that struggle to thine end,*
> *With not a friend to animate, and tell*
> *To other ears that death became them well*

Of all the stanzas on the two pages, my eyes focused on the above. Was this the fate of my lovers? The mystery saddens and deepens. One more time I so very carefully turned the pages to find any more hidden writings. Yes, there was one more, on the last blank page before the end of book advertisements. It was a different handwriting. It was hers, I know now, with the front inscription the shy young man, hesitant to express his feelings. She expressed hers powerfully.

*Today my love flies low over the earth like a swallow
before rain, and touching the tops of the flowers has
culled you these. Kiss them until they open, they are
full of my thoughts as the world, to me, is full of you.*

I quickly closed the book. Caught, peeking into the
heart and very soul of a lovesick young lady. Or maybe an
old woman remembering through watery eyes times long,
long ago. But regardless of their fate, I will remember the
beginning. The friend who dared not express thoughts of
poetry, but expressed his love, emotion, the romance and
the beautiful. And he did it more powerfully than Byron
could have imagined. Then her passionate response, blind
to all but him and the gentle, flower filled world they lived
in. I know that love continues to this day and will last as
long as the aspen flutters in the breeze. And as long as
blue gentians paint the alpine meadows, this love passes
overhead with each wisp of cloud on every July afternoon.

METHUSELAH

When I first saw him, I immediately thought of an old gnarled juniper growing out of a sandstone cliff amidst red desert sands stretching to the horizon. Or an ancient windswept bristlecone pine standing on a lonely mountaintop, half-dead branches reaching for the stars. His hair was pure white and full, his skin weathered and leathery like that of an old tortoise. He wore bib overalls and a white shirt. It was practical and comfortable, the uniform of a man of the land, a man unconcerned with what others might think of him. He was ninety if he was a day, but he was spry and full of life. Yet when I looked in his crystal blue eyes, it was like looking back in time. They were young, full of interest, but lonely. The loneliness overpowered me. He was beyond his time, alone, drifting. He radiated a sorrow and sadness that is found only in the last of a kind.

He had shown up at the open house for the Mendocino National Forest centennial. How appropriate. Today's 100-year-old bureaucracy was young when he was. When he explored and played as a youth, the promise of the new concept of preserving a forest was just beginning. Young men bet their future on an idea. Their world was new, the natural surroundings needed saving from the ravages of the greed and impatience of a young state and young nation. These men built roads and trails, marked timber sales, fought fires, catered to the rich city tourists from San Francisco and Sacramento.

He watched the short movie celebrating the past

hundred years. I watched him as he gazed in rapt
attention, his feet lightly tapping to the music of Enya,
then of bluegrass. An occasional smile cracked his lips;
his thoughts intrigued me. What was his world? Did he
recognize the faces of the young fire lookouts, the old
rangers, people now long turned to dust? What was
his connection to this experiment called the California
National Forest? Did he sweat and labor as a young man in
a remote CCC camp? Did he help build roads in the early
forest, fight fire, build trails, herd sheep? Did he hike the
remote canyons in search of grizzly or bighorn?

I would never know and part of me didn't want to
know. He was like a turtle sticking his neck out of his shell.
He lived in a world not my own and even asking him could
be an intrusion. But the other part of me needed to know.
His loneliness told me he wanted to share it. How does the
last one standing share something that no one else could
possibly know?

After the short movie, he walked the hallway looking
at the historic pictures lining the corridors of the office
building. I followed him, wondering how to ask him my
questions. After he had gazed at the first few pictures, I
asked if he recognized any faces. He said no. Then I saw
the timeless gaze of his blue eyes. They were looking
past me, past the pictures. He said rather softly that he
was looking for a man named Bidwell, or something
like that. He knew him long ago, but lost track, decades
ago. As he said that, his voice softened, turned wistful.
"Probably died like we all do." Had most of his world died?
He pointed to a man in another picture, a forest ranger
from the first decade of the forest. "I knew his daughter."
Then he smiled, a smile that told me volumes. He had
fond memories of the daughter. But memories were all he

had left. I invited him to look at the rest of the pictures, dozens of them, lining the walls. He disappeared down the corridor, lost in time. When I saw him minutes later, I asked if he saw any more people he knew. He smiled that lost, lonely smile, and said no.

We are all unique, knowing a world belonging to each of us alone and known to no one else. I am not there yet, standing on that point on the mountain top where the wind blows my white hair, chafing my furrowed turtle skin. I am not of the club yet, that group that has lost most of its members. That old white headed man of the earth who has watched his youth race away from him, watched his friends die, his loves disappear into the soil. Is there sorrow? Regret? Can he see what is next? He, and others like him, know and cannot tell someone like me. It was his world, not mine. I hadn't the right to know and he did not have the ability to tell.

I watched him walk out the door, back into his shell, into his world. He will be gone soon and who will mourn? Maybe family. Surely the mountains, the streams, the wind, the trees, older than he. Mourn may not be the correct word. Welcome to the secret fraternity of souls, celebrate, laugh.

I silently thanked him for coming, sharing what he could, although most of his knowledge remained unspoken. I didn't know his name and never would. Names are so unimportant for people, places, things. When we name them, we lose our ability to see them clearly. We don't ask questions any longer. We think we know them but we don't. We should continue to question until we close our eyes for the last time. At that time, our questions begin to be answered.

I would leave this brief fire assignment soon and go

back to my home a thousand miles away, never to see him again, at least in this life. But I would hear his sigh, his long unspoken dreams in the wind. The clouds passing overhead would whisper his name as the hint of rain or snow over the horizon turned into reality. I would see him again as I looked into the mirror in the distant future. Then I would understand. I would know the password into his world. It would then be my world as well.

Interlude: Prairie Thunderstorm

The Illinois morning of my youth was hot,
August mornings usually were.
Steamy summer air, hazy blue skies.
A blue jay scolding the world from his treetop perch.

Sounds of cicadas,
Or were they just crickets and other buggy things,
That filled the air with sound waves,
Muffled through the dampness.

By afternoon, the stillness competed with the stifling heat
For sensory saturation.
You felt it coming. Ominous and threatening.
Off to the west, as much as one could see west.

They appeared as mountains of cloud,
Building, boiling, roiling upwards.
White turning to grey to blue, then purple.
It filled the sky, it filled your being.

It was sudden, with little warning.
Sometimes the TV put a little symbol on the bottom
      of the screen.
But in those early days, who watched TV?
Especially on an August afternoon.

You heard the first rumble off in the distance.
A faint boom, could have been a railroad car bumping the next.
Fast freights passed by the house throughout the day and night.
But this was no train. The sounds came closer.

You looked into the darkening sky, awed by cloud tops
Stretching halfway to the moon. But there was no moon.
The lightning lit the backsides of the dark clouds.
The wind hit like one of those fast freights of the B & O.

Birds streaked by, turned and hovered, wings outstretched
    in the gale.
They knew no fear. They knew wind.
Branches swayed, leaves broke loose, chasing the birds.
Dirt and candy bar wrappers swept over the ground.

The first raindrops pattered slowly, then more quickly.
It was fun to stand, head turned upwards.
Catch a raindrop, earn a point.
No fun when it hit the eye and not the mouth.

Lightning followed by thunder. Count the seconds.
Seven, or was it five, I never could remember.
A mile away, safe to play.
Count to three, time to flee.

We knew when to run inside.
If we were on a bike, we flew with the birds
To get home before the fury hit.
Blackness brought the panic.

Safely inside, we stood wide eyed.
Lightning, boom of thunder; echoes filled the room.
Rain came in buckets, pounding, splashing.
Puddles rose from the dirt, rivers ran along the sidewalks.

A flash, the power went off, a tree down over a power line.
Thunder filled our ears. We laughed, covering fear.
Was this how Noah felt?
Hail signaled the end. It bounced off the roof, deafening
      us more than thunder.

The sky lightened, the wind eased.
Suddenly the pitter and patter of light raindrops
Turned to drips falling off trees.
The thunder disappeared to the east, trailing a lighter
      grey of thin clouds.

Blue sky, cool air, a freshness cleansed by ozone.
We slowly eased outside.
Water still ran down the street, seeking the storm drains.
Puddles deep enough to swim in.

But mothers always said keep out, you will be sucked down
Into the hidden sewers of the underworld,
Full of demons and witches.
Watch it gurgle and disappear, but stay away.

The birds sang again, invigorated,
Crickets temporarily silenced.
Already the nightcrawlers were covering the ground,
Splaying themselves in drowned pity on the sidewalks.

Baseball game rained out today.
Go to the schoolyard and play.
We explored the damage, trees down, limbs covering streets.
Just another August thunderstorm in 1955, another day.

Provide the sultry for tomorrow's humid blast.
Clean the branches, pile in the alley.
Wait for the mud to dry so we can walk in the garden.
Tomatoes need picked, weeds grew overnight.

Interlude: Mendocino

Mendocino
The name opens a world of imagination.
The adjective of Mendoza,
Viceroy of 16th century New Spain.

He lives forever
as a wild coast, a cape, a county.
Today, he is a National Forest.
Surely the least in the thoughts of the Viceroy.

He may have seen the coast,
from a ship bouncing on the waves of his peaceful sea
that stopped his empire to the west.
Or maybe not.

Mendocino.
It has a poetic ring.
The aura of wildness.
I prefer the coast over the forest.

Both are wild and untamed.
One belongs to the sea, endless, poetic itself.
One is rooted to the land, the mountains.
That is where we live, walk, manipulate.

Viceroy Mendoza would have avoided the forest.
It was steep, crowded by manzanita, oak, pine.
Patrolled by grizzly, puma, rattlesnakes.
Cleansed by fire, flood.

Much more interesting than the sea,
But is it?
Solid but changing; so is the coast.
Full of life, as is the shore.

Offering hidden dangers, hidden prizes.
So do the waves crashing on the cliffs.
How is it different?
We will not use the word 'better'.

Always there, never discovered,
Although in our arrogance,
We proudly discover everything.
People lived there long before the Viceroy offered his name.

Not as long as the puma, the eagle, the bear.
They hung on as the mountains rose,
Riding high into the air, staying at the foot of the trees.
The sea breeze died before it reached here.

Mountains folded, rivers eroded.
Lightning thundered, fires burned,
Trees grew in quiet majesty.
Birds painted the sky, soaring with the clouds.

The subjects of the Viceroy
Lived with the land,
Saved the heathen,
Thought of the old country, the old life.

Only when the call of oro
Fired the madness of greed
Did life change.
As life changed, the mountains did too.

Long before Smokey threw his first bucket of water,
The natives lit their first fire.
Watching the magic of lightning,
They understood that flames were good.

They cleared the brush,
that brought in the deer.
Fire meant life, smoke did too.
Life was easy, so was death.

Señor Mendoza left a legacy,
Not by actions, but name only.
His subjects either feared or revered him.
No one now remembers him.

But they know his coast, his cape, his forest.
The word has a thousand meanings,
A million memories in ten million lives.
Mendocino. Close your eyes.

THE END OF TIME

Time is the image of eternity

Diogenes Laertes,
Lives and Opinions of Eminent Philosophers

———•—•—•———

We must welcome the future,
Remembering that soon it will be the past,
And we must respect the past,
Remembering that once it was all
That was humanly possible.

George Santayana, *Apologia Pro Mente Sua*

AUTUMN

The autumn day was another perfect one. October had been warm and dry with only a few frosty mornings and a couple of light showers. No blustery days of snowy winter previews had sullied the daydream weather. The colors had been crystal sharp, with the yellows and golds of roses, cottonwoods, and grasses mixing with the reds and oranges of the sumacs. Now, nearing the onset of November, the leaves were slowly dropping to carpet the forest floor. The light breeze would loosen a few more, as the branches stood with their bare skeletons to hang silently awaiting the first snow. The cattails had not yet released their seeds to float in the breeze, but that was soon to come.

I stood along the creek, listening to the gurgle and chuckle of the flowing water tunnel through the drooping grasses and watercress. I also listened to the comical mumblings of the magpie, chirps and clucks interspersed with some silly babbling. Maybe she understood her language, but it only brought a smile to my baffled face. The black as midnight ravens soaring overhead made a more dignified squawk, but still an annoying announcement that they ruled the air, not their long-tailed white splotched smaller cousin. As usual, the juncos and towhees scrambled in the sumac tangles, hopping from branch to ground and back. They always looked busy and not quite sure what they were doing or where they were going. The chickadee came to see if I had a sunflower seed as he perched upside down, chattered at me, then flew off in a huff.

I quietly looked around at the scene, trying to enhance every sense I could use to capture the symphony of life around me. I spotted a couple of deer higher up the hillside as they watched me carefully, not moving an inch until they were confident I was no threat. Their noses twitched effortlessly, telling them more about me than I even knew myself. As I started to walk slowly along the trail, we played peek-a-boo through the brambles of branches and roses. They moved on, following me but slowly easing uphill, leaving me to ponder their thoughts. A bunny scurried into the mass of sumac where no one else could possibly penetrate. He was as silent as the stillness itself. He had a safe hidey hole, quite comfortable for him, I imagined.

During all this, I could sense no other trace of humanity in my sanctuary along the creek. No other noises, no sights, nothing human, except my own being. I was immersed in nature, exactly what I wished, alone with myself, but still only a few minutes and few hundred yards from the comfort of my house. I enjoyed it but wondered if there were many others who would feel this contentment. Sadly, I felt there weren't, at least among anyone under thirty or maybe forty, even fifty years old. What were people losing by distancing themselves from a scene like this? I needed no cell phone, no text messages, no conversation in any way except with the deer and magpies. Humans had become so separated from our natural setting, we were becoming something alien to life itself.

Another breeze wafted along the creek, releasing more red leaves to float and scatter to the ground. A mottled carpet of yellow, brown, and red was expanding in its effort to protect a ground preparing for freezes and snow. We all hoped for a deep white blanket this year. We usually did in this droughty climate.

A cold front was forecast to blow through the area later that night. A few outlier clouds and stronger breezes were slowly encroaching. I watched the increasing flutter of small red sumac leaves. I knew our perfect autumn was coming to a close. This was an annual event, with the outcome known. Only the timing and intensity might change year to year. It climaxed the shutting down of life for some. First the hummingbirds left, then the juncos arrived. The big bucks slowly filtered down from the high country; the first freeze put our garden to bed. Now the turning and falling of the leaves left only the first snow to signal a rapidly approaching frozen winter solstice.

I wanted this moment to last, but with a sadness of endings, I knew it was time. By tomorrow, we would wake up to nearly bare tree limbs, a cold wind, white-topped peaks of the high country. I would prefer a shocking blow such as a few inches of snow. Then, there would be no question that autumn had turned into winter, but I knew we would be given tantalizing regressions of warm days before the cold and white took possession for good. Then I would walk my deserted forested hillsides enjoying the brisk cold, the ice-lined creeks. Winter had its own serendipitous moments that took a little more courage and effort than a day like this. Each season had its treasures and I was basking in the golden glow of an autumn soon to end.

I sat on a rock, as I tend to do when I wish to grasp

larger meanings. I pondered the colorful mass of lichens, orange and grey, green and tan. They knew no seasons, but they were the definition of time that I was searching for. Time, that elusive passage of seasons, seemed to leave the lichens alone. To my limited eyesight, they stayed the same, year after year, decade after decade, showing only a slow spread, a slight change in their amoeba shape. They did put up spores or whatever passed for their reproductive process, but it was so subtle, I never noticed it. Was this what time meant? A slow progression, but something only the rocks notice. Another season to me meant a slow march towards some end. An end to me, but nothing meaningful to the lichen, the hillside, the rocks.

The traditional meaning of winter was that of death, endings, sleep, transformations. Of course, springtime would mean new life, resurrections, renewal. But why should winter and death mean an ending? Endings were nothing more than part of beginnings, a piece of the circle, the cycle of life. There was no end, only a transformation, a change, the cleaning of old in order to prepare the new.

Humans have misunderstood time. We count years, birthdays, anniversaries, seasons, lives by the hour and minute. I stood up and touched an ancient juniper. I could count the rings and tell how old it was in years. But its atoms had been around since some long lost sun exploded billions of years ago. Did we count them? Age and death only rearranged the life that surrounds us. So why did I come down the hillside to say goodbye to the life now reassessing itself? Maybe it had more to do with my own uncertainty, my lack of understanding of my place in this grand display of life.

Heaving a sigh of my never-ending confusion and lack of understanding, I said goodbye nevertheless. The year was one more in a procession of life, including death, that left an endless trail behind me. Maybe next year, I might understand it a little better. If not, then I would enjoy the colors, the sounds, the shapes, the smells of life itself. I could live with that.

The Grave

I wonder if he knows that I am standing here today. The small simple tombstone states that "Lloyd Albert Johnson, born May 1902, died August 1967," lies here under the grass and wildflowers.

I have no idea who Lloyd Albert Johnson was. I doubt if there are a lot of people alive today in 1985 who know, or who care. I get too dizzy wandering through the vacuum of the cosmos thinking about the absolute insignificance of the meaning or the life of any individual, including myself. I will leave that wondering for an icy, starlit night.

For now, I'm sure that Lloyd Albert must certainly rest in peace overlooking a place he had some attachment to. From here, guarded from the searing heat of today by a fir and a grove of old yellow bark pines, he watches the passing seasons of Clover Valley. We are miles from a highway, miles from what we call civilization. No one lives out here. No one, that is, but the jays and mice and coyotes. Maybe Lloyd Albert had more attachment to them than to anyone else.

He could have belonged to the old abandoned ranch sitting a few hundred yards below us at the bottom of this gently sloped hill; he could have been struggling to raise a few cows, a little hay, and whatever else this land would allow. He could have been one of the hundreds of loggers who for a generation or two searched this wilderness for timber. Those trees probably consisted of huge old yellow bark Jeffery pines, now all but gone from the nearby forest. That lost forest was an open grown, park-like forest sheltering a line of rails from a narrow gauge logging railroad, now as forgotten as the giant pines.

By the care that someone has given to a strong and durable fence around this site, I must assume someone else rests here also. A single lonely grave would not take up this much space. Lloyd Albert has this whole valley. I'm sure he wouldn't want his final resting place to be so imposing. Maybe it's his parents who might have originally homesteaded this wilderness so far from their birthplaces. Maybe brothers who preceded him by a full lifetime. Or grandparents who followed the guidance of old Jim Beckworth a century and more ago and pioneered this outpost of the Sierra.

His soul left his body nearly twenty years ago, but I'm sure his memory of this view must stretch back almost to his birthday that June day, four days short of seventy-five years ago. It is a little sad that Lloyd Albert was only 55 when he died. Even then, that was not a ripe old age. Either he worked himself to an early death, or a terrible accident claimed his life earlier than he wished. A century ago, a death at 55 might not have been so early. Now we are living longer but not necessarily better. His life might have been simpler, but he still witnessed a big change during this century. I have so much I wish to ask him.

Was he born in that house below us? That large two-story farm house is silent now with boarded up windows. That tombstone of a house was once as alive as Lloyd Albert, with noises of yelling children and clanging pans, men branding the calves and later dining in a big open dining room on Rocky Mountain oysters after a hard and long day in the corral across the road. I can hear the sounds of that evening—the iron pot being clanked down on the hot wood stove, the scraping of tarnished forks on the cracked china plates, the hearty laughing of the men, the embarrassed admonitions of the ladies. Young Albert picking up the scratched fiddle and trying to make those sophisticated sounds to impress the even younger Emma Lou. The crickets and cicadas chirping loudly outside. Their sounds bring me back to their descendants of a half century later.

The buzzing flies and ever present chickadees leave me no silence now as I look over the valley. It must be a peaceful difference here in the depth of January, as the snow lies indifferent to the grass and sage. Did Lloyd Albert stand here on the edge of a February blizzard and contemplate the scene?

Why is it that Gandalf, my dog and companion, is so attracted to the grave marker? He is fascinated by something. I continually call him away. I'm sure it must the mouse that probably lives under the stone. Or could it be some feeling of the presence of Lloyd Albert himself. I can't see spirits. Maybe Gandalf can.

I'd like to think that Lloyd Albert is here seeing what this June day is like at Clover Valley in 1985. He is certainly here through my eyes. And the other people lying here at my feet? I cannot leave them out. But they left me out. They blend into the land as easily as the pine needles. I think I respect them even more than Lloyd Albert. Their memory was left in the minds of those they left behind. Maybe Lloyd Albert was one they left behind. Did their memory die with Lloyd Albert? Someone couldn't quite let Lloyd Albert go so completely, though I imagine he might have preferred it that way.

I certainly would like to spend my forever in a way like this, only not here. I've my own Clover Valleys I'd like to overlook. But quietly, with no marker but a stately old yellow bark pine, or maybe a grove of graceful aspen dancing yellow in the October twilight.

Whatever Lloyd Albert knew and loved about this place, he will keep with him till eternity, sharing with no one who chances by like I did. He holds it until the last snow blankets the valley in front of us. I kind of like it that way. As I'm sure does Lloyd Albert.

New Year's

It is an annual occurrence, taken quite seriously by
some, rather amusingly by me. The new year, which
quite properly should begin on the winter solstice, or
even on the summer solstice, somehow was relegated to
that artificial date of January 1. It involves reflections on
the new year, reminiscences on successes and failures,
resolutions and promises of conquests, charity and
goodness that abounded like falling autumn leaves.
A week or two after the partying (a flimsy reason to
celebrate) and the somber promises to live a better life,
the daily routine and character flaws return as usual.

I resolve there is no new year. There is no change of
this false invention of man-time. Life struggles on under
the same frozen sky, the same warming sun, now hanging
longer every day in its effort to return to life from its
winter ordeal.

What is this measurement of that mystical
undiscovered dimension of time? We scientifically
calculate to the minutest, ultimately insignificant detail.
We schedule our days in this false division of time. In
losing reality with the delicate and intricate changing of
shadows and passage of seasons, we are imprisoned to the
dictatorship of the clock.

Revolution is in order. I resolve to join the daily
procession of the sun god in its timeless path. I will
ignore the calendar and its monotonous numbers. By
the calculations of the squirrel, I shall determine time by
season. The time to thicken my fur, if only I could, and

plan for the austere days of ice and wind, the time to
welcome the warmth of spring, come at last, and days
of abundance.

I shall live not for a magic number on a dial, but rise
before the sun, await its colorful light show of arrival, learn
to read its shadows. And even after it has faded past its
discovery of the horizon, I can read the display of stars, the
face of the moon.

And oh, the frustration of a cloudy day. The confusion
of a snowstorm, when all is a mystified guess. But there are
ways, I suppose. Or does time really stand still? Life cannot
be all ordered and certain. Only man dares insult himself
by such a trick.

This celebration called the New Year is a paradox,
for we praise ourselves for weathering one and cheer
ourselves for success in the one to come. We celebrate this
thing called time when we are as lost to its meaning as we
are to our own meaning.

Time is nature and the natural world. When we lose
touch with nature, then we have lost touch with time. Thus
we invent this clock time. Look around you. How many
people wear wrist watches? Nearly everyone I see. I have
not worn one for decades. I do steal glances at clocks, so
I am as guilty as most, but when outside, which is most
of the time when possible, I try to figure out the time
by looking at the sun. I am usually close, but I am also
not tied to getting anything done by clock time. I have
the luxury to spend time doing what needs done, then
stopping when my body says it is time to stop. Body time,
now that is what we need to focus on.

What is one day, but an endless repeat of the one
before? An infinity of variations so subtle, we cannot
comprehend the difference. But what a crime that we,

in our arrogance, are unable to comprehend that each day is a masterpiece in time, that mystic dimension that may repeat all factors in combinations so alike, but never to occur again. Each day is a sacred symphony of light and wind and heat, clouds and shadows and noise—all combined with time in a kaleidoscope we call life. Ever changing and never-ending time, shared with every living thing that has ever existed. Ever and never. Now there are concepts to ponder and celebrate. Happy New Year.

THE ROOT CELLAR

For some reason, I felt guilty as I stood looking into the root cellar, that legacy of Hazel the old hermit. I was now protector and restorer of the land she lived on as a recluse for so long. Yet I felt I was somehow betraying Hazel as I uncovered a part of her life hidden by years of neglect. I had spent days clearing junk from the area around the root cellar, but I had to do this first in order to be able to even get to the roof. Then I shoveled a ton or more of old dirt, coal ashes, rocks, and who knows what other microscopic debris off the roof. This also made me feel guilty since deer had periodically used this soft dirt as a bed.

No longer. The dirt was piled around the cellar where junk used to be; the pieces of corrugated metal strips, metal car parts, and pieces of cardboard that served as the final sheathing to hold the dirt were stacked in separate piles of burnable and non-burnable. Then the old boards, slabs of logs, and finally logs had come off. Sunlight on this bright spring morning shone into the formerly dank and dark cellar, light touching jars and bottles for the first time in decades. Hazel's secrets and parts of her private life now lay exposed.

I had been probing Hazel's secrets for years. Or, more accurately, trying to. Hazel's lonely, hermit life was one big mystery and most answers followed her to her grave. But I was persistent. I knew that things lay hidden in this root cellar. Parts of the roof and sides had long ago caved in and in my earlier research on Hazel, I had been told that she had old brass lanterns and other valuable things stored in her root cellar that were long ago abandoned when the small cave-ins had started. The damage was evident. Dirt covered everything and some shelves were totally buried. I surveyed the remnants of this once proud cellar as I shuddered with dismay of the task of digging through this midden. I had done the preliminary work to get to the archeological site. Now my real work of discovery lay before me.

But why did I feel guilty? As I had done many times before, I was standing outside looking in a window of Hazel's life, long ago turned to dust. I was a peeping Tom. She would never have allowed me to get this close. Hazel was the ultimate private person, yet I persisted in peering into her window as she stood exposed before me. Digging through her cellar was invading the most private parts of her. I would see what she ate, what she saved, what she stored in this, the sole bank vault of her life's possessions.

I would not be able to tell how orderly she was. Order was long ago turned to chaos by falling dirt, pack rats, ground squirrels, and the erosion of time. Entropy at work, down here in the bowels of the earth, although rather shallow bowels at that.

As I gazed down on the few jars exposed on the top layer of dirt, I spotted a Ball Mason jar that didn't look right. I cautiously stepped down into the cellar for my preview search and picked up the jar. It was a half-gallon jar. I had never seen such a thing before. I carefully picked it up and carried it outside, my first prize discovery. What more lay hidden in this dusty jumble?

Stepping carefully over the pile of metal and wood that was the result of my unroofing of the cellar, I stopped and looked around me. The cellar was in what would have been the side yard of the old homestead cabin, whose east wall was only a few feet away. I was right outside the window, looking into her bedroom as I worked. I knew she was watching me, unable to do anything to stop me. Walt was somewhere out back, mending a fence, or stretching barbed wire onto one of his make-shift fences that was to give me heartburn years later.

I chuckled as I thought of Walt carefully raiding his own personal auto graveyard to find pieces of car doors and folding hood covers from cars that I probably had never heard of. He laid these, interwoven with corrugated sheets of metal to cover the board slabs that he undoubtedly picked through from some long abandoned sawmill. Some of the metal was totally rusted into shreds, while other pieces were remarkably whole and usable. However, I would not play Walt and try to reuse these. They were bound for the dump. I was unceremoniously tossing them into a pile, something that probably would cause Walt heartburn as he watched me make quick work of dismantling his rather effective roof. It did last decades and served well to keep summer rains and winter snows from penetrating into the dark recesses of their pantry.

I had to duck as I worked the north end. The old apricot tree, leaning perilously to the east and somehow still alive, was hanging low over the roof area. The tree was half dead, but new blossoms were just days away from covering the tree with pink and white flowers. This tree, probably a product of a pit spit out by Walt as he lazed outside on some summer afternoon, had weathered the history I longed to discover. It guarded the root cellar and added color for well over half a century. It now clung to survival, hidden by brambles and roses gone wild. Around its base were scattered the dump of old pipe, rusted metal, broken

jars, chicken wire. The dignity of a beauty among trash—
was this symbolic of Hazel? I'd yet to see the beauty in her,
but then, I didn't know her and I have struggled to look for
something beautiful in her.

Standing here on this spring morning, with apricots
ready to blossom, grass greening up, bluebirds and wrens
singing arias to the sky, I did see the beauty that she must
have seen. Surely, she did keep the weeds out of her yard.
Surely, she could have walked around the house without
struggling through the brambles and tripping over junk.
I had to think that. I had to believe that only in her final
years did she succumb to total sloth. Time has a way of
adding to apathy, or maybe just trying to cover it up.

I tried to picture Hazel walking out on a day like this
to get a jar of apricot jam, stored neatly on the shelf of her
food vault. She would have paused to listen to the wren
warbling his heart out. She would have seen the irises
breaking green into the sunlight. She would have seen
the ermine, now mottled brown and white as he scurried
under the outhouse. She would have felt the breeze as it
blew warmth in from the south, just ahead of the March
streaks of clouds that just might bring a few drops of rain
down here, snow flurries higher up.

Only towards the end, did she fill cardboard boxes with
every jar she emptied. I have seen this evidence already,
as I noticed the few jars and bottles sticking up out of the
dirt, the flotsam bobbing on the surface of a dusty rubble
sea. But then, as evidenced by the hillside garbage dump, it
did seem like she saved everything she ever purchased or
borrowed. This was a person—I had a hard time referring
to her as a lady—who was on the edge of survival most of
her life. She was a child of want, refugee of the Depression,
victim of hard times, a recluse who shunned civilization.

Maybe she did save everything. All that deserved better than the hillside dump, went down there, in the root cellar.

Carefully sifting through decades of accumulation, I would find out more but I would still not find out who she really was. Were the whiskey and wine bottles hers or Walt's? Did she can her food, or did her mother or other relatives do it for her? Would I find the old brass lanterns, or was that some myth told to add to her mystery? Was it another myth that she probably hid what little money she had in a jar somewhere, either buried in the root cellar, or buried in a hole in the ground, to forever lie in wait of discovery?

I took a breath, crouched over and ducked into the cellar. Shafts of light filtered through the apricot tree above, past the shelves half covered in dirt, through the exposed glass of jars and bottles. Dust motes filled the air. I knew what I would find and very little of it would be worth saving. As I carefully lifted jars, dirt jostled to fill in gaps on the shelf. More dirt sifted down from the sides of the cellar once again covering a good Mason jar, dozens of old empty ketchup bottles, broken jars, old metal canning jar lids, broken slabs of wood.

I had to surface every few minutes to get a breath of fresh air. As I poked my head up, a big-eyed doe wandered by, looked at me and wondered what kind of strange looking badger had popped up out of this hole. I glanced again at the far off mountains, still capped with a snowy cover. I looked again at the piles of trash surrounding the cellar. I knew this was a futile effort but I had to do it. The spirit of Hazel urged me on, at the same time cursing my presence. It would be a slow process, but I had the time. Time was about all I would find, time that hid years of loneliness, seclusion, secrets of a lonely old lady. Time forever shrouded in mystery.

CHRISTINE'S STORY

Christine Anderson was born in 1876 and died in 1903. She kept secrets well since that is all I know about her. Other than that she had some connection to Rawlins, Wyoming, since that is where she is buried.

Someone must have thought a lot of Christine; she has a very elaborate headstone, a large vertical slab of granite, simple, yet elegant in its roughness, with a beautifully carved lily flower. I will visualize Christine this way—elegant, but rough around the edges. She was young when she died and did not have the time to develop into a polished elegance. I imagine this was hard to do in turn-of-the-century Rawlins. With no offense intended to the good people of Rawlins, I imagine it is hard to do still today. Rawlins itself could be described as rough around the edges yet with some glimpses of hidden elegance. It is a shady oasis surrounded by windswept plains. Sort of like a slab of granite with a larger than life lily carved on it.

Katherine and I are sitting here now on a frozen April day in the aftermath of a spring blizzard. The snow drifts have sculpted the ground to complement Christine's headstone. The leafless trees of the cemetery throw their shadows on the drifted snow. The large cottonwoods etch their spiderweb shadows in jagged array over the broken surface of the snow near the headstone. Some of the trees seem as old as Christine would be today. I wonder if as a young girl, she knew these trees as saplings. Did she come here to play in this park-like setting?

The trees and Christine have drawn us like a magnet

on our recent journeys through Rawlins. We've experienced the colors of autumn leaves and the cool shade of a hot July afternoon. As the dog wanders among the headstones sniffing for unseen spirits, we enjoy our sandwiches for lunch. We now make a ritual of stopping here three or four times a year as we take this route from South Dakota to western Colorado. The circumstances of our first meeting escape me, lost in the immensity of this Wyoming landscape. But we look forward to our visits with Christine. Her silence tells us a lot as we sit and think of her.

From our picnic spot near her grave, we can see the refinery at East Sinclair, a few miles to the east of Rawlins on I-80. There was a more recent death there, on a late summer night in 1967: the Pink Phinque. My first car, a 1957 Ford, was carrying me nonstop from Idaho home to Illinois in late August. With a nearly broken arm, after a hectic summer of forestry camp and a short job working seven days a week at the state park in McCall, I was going home before returning to Idaho to continue college. Forgetting to add oil at the last gas fill up set the stage for the engine to simply freeze up and die, probably at about the closest point of the journey to this grave. The car limped as far as the East Sinclair exit, where it gasped its last breath and died. There it sat for several years, with our last view of it in the early 1970s. It no longer sits there, but the truck stop where it was parked no longer exists either. Death comes easily in this part of Wyoming, but life does go on. I wonder if Christine somehow carelessly forgot to add her oil, or life's equivalent.

We could stop in Rawlins someday and go to the local newspaper and do some research on Christine. Or check with the historical society or county archives. It might be easy to find out more about Christine. Was she born in

this brand new railroad town back in '76 or did she come
west on the train? Did she even live in Rawlins, or was she
visiting? What kind of family did she leave? Was she pretty
or educated or love fine flowers, such as lilies? So much
to find out. But so much should remain unknown, for we
feel much more comfortable talking to a Christine who is
as unknowable as this part of the high plains. Life needs
to contain mysteries. Within that mystery, the unknowns
can take on the beauty they may not have actually had.
Christine will be forever young, carefree and headstrong,
ready to tame this wild new land. She will be a beautiful
and elegant lady still rough at the edges. She somehow
knows that she helped set the stage for a movement that
changed this land. She left it to us and now we need to
figure out what she wanted to achieve.

So many questions, but we must travel on now,
Christine, for we have several hours yet to go today. We are
on our way to fulfill our dreams, a chance you probably
did not have. We will stop by again to chat and to just sit
and enjoy the cool breeze in this green oasis. You have
a wonderful spot. May you rest in peace, but be careful
about giving up your secrets. Secrets are all you have left.
Along with a slab of granite, rough hewn yet adorned with
an elegant lily flower.

THE CEMETERY

My search for the early history of the town of Hotchkiss took some strange turns at the start. On a blustery March morning, I stopped in the Hotchkiss Museum to visit Ellen and Elaine, the dedicated local historians. While waiting for Ellen to help a repairman figure out why the alarm system had been going off in the museum (answer: probably wind whistling through the cracks around doors and windows, although I'm not sure Elaine bought this explanation), I examined a faded chart on the wall. It seemed to be a list of names penciled in rectangles in rows. Most of the pencil work was fading to a point of near illegibility. Some names were inked in. My first guess was the location of plots in a cemetery.

Sure enough, when I asked Ellen what this was, she said it was the original Hotchkiss cemetery. I didn't even know where the new cemetery was, much less the original, so I asked where the old one was. Above the new one, of course. After she tried to describe how to get there, I politely acted like I knew where it was (I didn't, but in a small town like Hotchkiss, it couldn't be hard to find). Then in order to make conversation, I mentioned that I was surprised the name of Duke was not listed on the chart. The Duke store was one of the original businesses in Hotchkiss and this pioneer family seemed to be quite prominent in the research I had done to date.

She replied quite enthusiastically that she had a lot of information on the Dukes and proceeded to pull out

several file folders of Duke correspondence and research.
One thing I quickly learned about both Ellen and Elaine
was that they were excited about their work, enthusiastic
about helping and otherwise obsessed with who did what
and when, and which descendants were still around. I
found this attitude contagious, although I really lacked that
same interest in the families and genealogy. My interest
was in the spirits and the lives that were no longer on this
earth. This was a rather esoteric philosophical rambling
that probably lost the Ellen's and Elaine's in a fog. Actually,
these ramblings sometimes lost me in a fog as well. But
that mystery was fun for me—trying to see where in
that foggy mist of time these ramblings would lead. For
example, leading to the cemetery. I had to find it; the
attraction was magnetic.

I love to wander in old cemeteries since they contain
secrets that will rarely be discovered. They hide the
successes and failures of lives and meld all the stories into
a dull uniformity. Everyone is the same here. No matter
how much a man or woman conquered and discovered in
life, no matter how powerful or lowly they were, young
or old, rich or poor, they are all the same in a cemetery,
reduced to one common denominator.

I did find Riverside Cemetery with some wandering
and backtracking. The lower or newer cemetery is your
typical manicured park-like setting. I just followed the
gravel road as it wound through the recent inhabitants
and wound upward past the tool shed, onto a higher bench
of the mesa. As I crested the hill and saw the old stones,
I knew this was my kind of place. It was natural. No lawn
and pine trees and park feeling here. This was the raw
untamed land as it was when the people who now lay here
first found it, the final home to the settlers and explorers

who pioneered this area. Bare soil, native grasses, rocks. And a view to die for. Literally. This was the summit, looking down on town and on the newer cemetery below. It overlooked the river and the valley. The West Elks loomed to the east, the open mesas to the south. This was Colorado in all its expansive and majestic glory. Mountains and rivers and mesas and space. Lots of space and sky, and limitless time to enjoy it.

I didn't know anyone here. But then, no one was here in reality. Memories were here, but fading more every year. Soon, this hilltop would be just some unknown and anonymous gathering of stone where some old people lie buried. No names, no history, no meaning. But for now, it was a place of reverence for me. I tried to walk with respect between the graves, but it was hard to tell where the graves were. One small headstone was the hiding place of some squirrel or other furry creature. A large hole disappeared under it. I looked, almost expecting to see a bone or tooth or other grisly remnant lying in the hole or on the surface. The squirrel that lived there didn't know this was some early settler or beloved wife or missed infant baby. It was simply home under another rock. Dust to dust, as we all will find out.

I wandered among the stones. Paxton and Friend. Pagone, Ruble, and Bennett. Whitehorn and Riehl. Churchill (now "Asleep with Jesus" as engraved on the tombstone) died 1906. The names and dates by themselves told a history unknown to me. Zenas W. Martin, born 1869 and died 1901 was also Asleep with Jesus. He must have had concerned and loving descendants who added this extra touch to a piece of stone. I wonder if Zenas knew Mr. Churchill. They both have had plenty of time by now to wake up and get to know Jesus quite well. I'm sure there is

quite a happy crowd up there or out there or wherever they
now reside.

Wesley B. Robertson was born in 1908 and died in
1909. He at least lived long enough to have the honor of a
name on his little stone. His siblings lined up next to him
didn't get that much. Three in a row, "Baby Robertson
– 1893", "Baby Robertson – 1905", then Wesley. I didn't
notice the parent's stones nearby. Are they here? Or did
they move on to a new place to forget the memories of the
North Fork Valley? What a tragic history of lost children.
Did any Robertson make it to adulthood?

Like lost little lambs, these children haunt the hilltop.
As a matter of fact, the lambs carved onto the little
tombstones add a touch of drama to these lost tragedies.
Nancy Helen Parker, born October 31, 1892 and died July
9, 1900, had the lamb along with these fading lines etched
in the marble stone, "Our darling one hath gone before,
To greet us on the blessed shore." The stone maker surely
washed these finished stones with his tears as he chiseled
the last word. How can one look on this and not feel the
loss suffered by little Nancy's grieving parents?

Or grab onto the handkerchief for the tombstone of
little Edward Otis DeGraffenreid, son of Edward and Violet.
He died in 1906. A trap door on the side of this metal
"stone" displayed what was probably the funeral program.
Now faded, but holding up well to the years, it proclaimed
"His last words were: 'Oh Papa, I feel so good. I hear the
band playing. The music is so nice.'" How could Edward
and Violet stand such heart wrenching sorrow? Evidently
little Edward Otis didn't mind; he was enjoying his exit.

These pioneers were tough. They had to be. This was
a tough land, although the loss of children was much
more common in those days, in the city and wilderness

alike. Many young ones didn't make it. But they were to hold the door to heaven open for their parents who were left to brave the struggle going on down here. Like Little Fletcher, beloved son of Victor and Hattie Harpst. He died in 1899, "aged 3 years and 8 mths. Jesus has called our darling home. Safe, safe in Heaven". Fletcher didn't get a lamb, but he did have a bouquet of flowers carved on this stone. Victor and Hattie knew he was safe up there. They probably had things tougher and maybe not so safe and secure down here, but I'm sure they are with him now.

Dr. and Mrs. J. T. Myers didn't sing praises to wherever Baby Myers was. He died July 6, 1898, aged 9 months. At that time, Hotchkiss was an infant town, just like Baby Myers. Dr. and Mrs. Myers left these words for him, "A precious one from us has gone. A voice we loved is stilled. A place is vacant in our home which never can be filled." The lamb was lying on the stone and not looking up like some others. Did the good doctor feel guilty that he came to Hotchkiss to save lives but could not save the one most important to him? Maybe they would have felt better if they could have added something like his being safe up there. Grief is different for different people.

Marguerite, daughter of Albert and Anna White died at age 1 year, 1 day in 1906. The day after her first birthday. Was she sick on the only birthday she ever had? Albert and Anna were not poetic; they just said goodbye to "papa's wee girlie" and "mamma's pet." Their grief was no less than the others were, I am sure. They must have been simple and honest folks, straight to the point and got on with life. Did Mamma get to have another pet? I hope so.

The poems were not limited to the young ones, though. Andrew Jackson Seaman died on April 21, 1896. This early spring day over one hundred years later found the trees leafing out and the wildflowers adorning the hillside. He left on a day the world was awakening from a long winter. He had lived a good life, being "62 years, 11 months, and 2 ds". His family bade him farewell with the words, "Our father has gone to a mansion of rest to the glorious land by the deity blessed." He left a glorious land behind as well. He didn't get a lamb, but then, a man with a name like that might not take kindly to having his mansion guarded by a little lamb. After all, he could have been a cowman and those early cowmen didn't hanker well to being associated with sheep.

The adults left hints of other histories. Such as the Simpsons. This struck me since it hit closer to home. They were listed as "Pioneers of Redlands Mesa." I now live on Redlands Mesa. It can be seen three miles to the west from here. I am also researching that history now. I'm glad to know I can look up the name Simpson. After all, he lost his wife in 1913, but then lived on himself until 1946. He died at age 102. That has to be a full and rich history, but so much of it without his beloved wife.

There are a lot of military veterans here. Their stones are all alike and quite simple. The Army wasn't one for frills. They must have paid for the headstones. James Hutchinson, Co. 1, 96 Ill INF. No dates. Did he die in a war somewhere? Or was his service to the 96 Ill during the Civil War? Not knowing military terminology, I didn't know if this meant Third or Illinois. I prefer Illinois since I was born in Illinois. Was this some neighbor of my great grandparents who left the farm and moved west after serving his duty for old Abe and the Union? I know things were getting crowded back there, although if he was a farmer, leaving that rich, black Illinois soil for this rocky clay hardpan out here would have been a big come down.

Maybe that led to his death, although I'll never know how old he was or even when he died.

Did Mr. Hutchinson know JNO W. Cain who was in Co. K of the 40 Ill INF? JNO W. was resting next to Susan Cain, born 1843, died 1917. She was listed as "Mother". Was he father? When did he leave her? Did they migrate out here, away from family and friends to settle the wilderness, then for him to die and leave her as mother of a family without a father? Guess I won't know that one either.

Charles Stithem shocked the community on August 12, 1900 when at age 13 years, 10 months and 18 days, he drowned in the North Fork Gunnison River. He is now "At Rest." Sounds like he went to rest in the river on a hot August day. A teenager in the days when a teenager grew up fast. Was he horsing around with the guys and did something stupid? Or was he trying to catch fish for supper that night and got hit by lightning as an August thunderstorm roared over Black Canyon and caught him by surprise? Doesn't matter. He is at rest now. Where along the river did this tragedy happen? Things like that still happen today.

The stones or markers are interesting. Some are nothing but weathered remnants of old wooden tombstones rising out of the rocky soil. There are slabs of marble or limestone; there are polished granite stones that are dated 90 years ago but look brand new. Maybe they are. There were metal markers that looked like stone (patented Western White Bronze, Des Moines). One of these for Wiley Sheek had the words in the shape of tree logs. By the way, Wiley was 55 when he died in 1897, but he got a lamb. I hope Wiley was a sheepman. He probably can't be embarrassed as long as he is up there in a mansion or with Jesus.

The Ackers have their plot fenced with a metal railing. Were they afraid someone would be inconsiderate to Warren, died May 9, 1889? Maybe he just wanted his space. Lots of the pioneers were like that. That's why they came out here to settle this wilderness. Life was getting too crowded other places. I can buy that. I won't care if someone walks over my grave, although I don't really plan to share space in a cemetery. I know I can't be buried somewhere in the forest under a tree. They don't like you to do that. Don't know why, if that's where I prefer. So just scatter my ashes on a perfect Colorado October afternoon. Let the ashes join the twirling aspen leaves as they scatter to nourish the soil. And Warren, I will stay away from your fenced plot. I'll give you that much.

There remained many blank plots with no stone or anything to remind us who lies there. There have been recent burials, such as Edward Vincent Pagone, died April 15, 1997. His stone includes space for Rosamond, born 1920 and married to Edward in 1949. She is still with us and missing Edward greatly, I imagine. Will she be the last to join this group? I don't mean that to sound morbid, but few come up here now. Most go to the new cemetery down below, that manicured and crowded place. Enos Hotchkiss and the Dukes and Dents and many other pioneers who founded this little town lie down there. Does that carry more prestige? Not to me. I admire those who rest up here. There may be some deep philosophical meaning to the people who prefer to be apart from the crowd, in a little less artificial setting.

This early March afternoon added to the reflective feeling I had while walking here. It was the blustery type day you expect in early March. I stood facing the cutting wind, looking at the symphony of clouds pushing into the wall of mountains behind me. Curtains of sleet and rain and snow piled up against Lamborn, while a patch of blue peaked above the Uncompahgre Plateau to the west. Puffy gray blue cumulus mixed with veils and wisps of squalls exploding here, passing there, disappearing in the distance. This was indeed the raw wilderness these pioneers found, tamed, and then succumbed to.

The geese honking down on the river didn't know or care, nor did the red tailed hawk soaring with the wind over the mesa. This was just another cold, blustery day like many other late winter days. Which sooner or later would turn into bright sunny June days with flowers blooming and newborn deer wandering down by the river. In a place like this, days just merge with more days, passing seasons endless to the horizon.

I think the Pagones and their neighbors understand and would appreciate this. So the early secrets of Hotchkiss I was searching for remained for the time being. The secrets are held tightly in the grips of bony hands lying on the bony ribs of hardy pioneers lying here. I glanced to the west and saw another squall heading this way. Blue sky soon disappeared as hail and snow erased the mountains. Driving down into the new cemetery, I saw the headstones marking the Dukes, founders of a town and creators of generations of followers. They were a part of the reason this town is here and I need to know that.

As I drove out, for the first time in my life a thought crossed my mind. Am I inspecting my future home? I don't really believe in cemeteries and burials and all that ritual. But then, it is quite a view. There will always be a river down below, with geese honking during a blustery March squall. They are anxious for the ice to melt and for the journey of adventure they will soon embark on. And the hope that the next day will be sunny and warm, with the first hints of spring. Maybe they are just disturbed by some stranger wandering by, trying to uncover the secrets hidden in this rocky Colorado soil. Secrets that are not meant to be found, but that will remain until the next glacier plows the rock and soil into the distant sea.

Tragedy at the Owl Tree

The sun warmed the clear blue April sky, reawakening life, a springtime promise of growth, newness and hope. I walked the trails I had built, discovering the first pink phlox of spring, the first brilliant red paintbrush, even the first blue eyed grass. I flushed two mourning doves from their lone eggs in simple nests at eye level along Sleeping Cedar trail. The warmth and new growth invigorated me. As I circled back along Strider Ridge, I decided to visit the nest tree and check on the progress of Momma Owl. She had been on her nest for a few weeks and should by now have fluffy new chicks nestled under her warm feathers. We were like proud parents waiting to give her moral support and encouragement.

The owl tree, a large old juniper just below the Owl Pond, is not far from our house. For most of the past twenty years, the owl tree had hosted nesting great horned owls. Many times, we proudly watched owls on the nest, and young bundles of feathers and down perched on the branches as we all waited for the day they first flew. We even re-routed one trail that went under the tree before we realized the nest was there. For the past few years, the nest was abandoned. No owls, no chicks. We always heard owls in the area, but for some reason, they didn't nest here. Then, this year they returned. Papa sitting nearby, flying silently off when I approached. Momma, huddled on the nest, barely visible on top of the pile of twigs, her squinting eyes below pointed ear tufts. The owls seemed late in nesting this year, but for a couple weeks, we had carefully

monitored the nest, anxiously awaiting the downy heads
poking over the rim of twigs.

I slowly walked towards the tree, noticing Momma
wasn't in her usual place. Something seemed wrong. Then
I noticed a tan colored shape on a lower limb. At first, I
thought it might be a rabbit, hung in the pantry, to provide
tomorrow's breakfast. The slight breeze ruffled feathers,
not fur. I looked closer, with a foreboding that I was
looking at something I didn't want to see. It was Momma,
hanging silently, quietly. Unmoving, a trickle of blood on
the branch, drops of red on the soil ten feet below her. Feet
hung lifeless, feathers askew.

A tragedy of life that had passed into death swirled
around me like a cloud blotting out the sun. I silently
mouthed the words "No, no, it can't be." But it was. I
looked a few feet above her to the nest. No downy heads
poked up. I knew they never would. I didn't want to look,
although I knew the answer to my unasked question: they
would be with Momma, wherever she was winging off to,
in an owl afterlife.

What I was seeing wasn't right in my world of order
and springtime hope. I thought back a few years when I
found the dead mountain lion a few hundred yards down
this same creek. Then, a sense of profound, spiritual awe
moved me. The power that lion symbolized overwhelmed
me beyond sadness. It was not right that something so
powerful, full of a life that fed on death, should be dead.
Now, seeing the owl gave me an overwhelming sadness
knowing another predator could meet a violent and sudden
death, especially at a time she was bringing new life into
this world. This wasn't right, I kept mumbling to myself
as I held back a choking lump in my throat, eyes watering
with growing sadness. How could her life be snuffed out

for no apparent reason? Nothing had eaten the owl. What had happened?

Returning to the house, I told Katherine to come quickly, but gave her no clue. We had done this same thing when I found the lion years ago. I needed comfort, but we needed to see how all life works, not just the pretty cheerful things. Life comes with death as a companion; one cannot happen without the other. The owl, the big cat, the eagles, the smaller cats, we share this life with them all. Every day they kill and eat living, breathing things that have eyes that blink, ears that twitch. The lion does not lie down with the lamb. It eats the lamb; the owl eats the rabbit. But the owl cannot die, nor should the lion. They cannot die just as they bring new life into this world. But again, I gazed on the harsh truth. Nature doesn't care.

I boosted Katherine up into the tree. She slowly ascended, taking pictures of first Momma, then the nest. Yes, the chicks were dead; small, not more than a week old, still covered in white wispy down, the two were curled against each other, next to a half-eaten chipmunk. Unable to eat without Momma feeding them torn bits of flesh, they soon joined her. Only two days ago we both had walked by here, Momma hunkered down watching us silently, two unknown animals passing beneath her tree.

I inspected the base of the tree in widening circles, trying to find evidence of what had happened. My conclusion was a bobcat had probably tangled with Momma. Momma gave a valiant fight, chased off Bob, scratched and beaten, not knowing he had inflicted fatal wounds. He did not come back to finish her off. Or she might have eaten a poisoned prairie dog in some nearby field. We will never know. She took the deadly secret with her. The chicks knew even less than we did. Momma didn't feed them so they died. But what about Papa?

I didn't know, but maybe owls mate for life. Did he
come back to the scene of death? Why didn't he care for
the chicks? Did he mourn for her? Did he have feelings
of sadness, of concern for the babies? Once again, we
will never know. We must be careful about putting our
emotions on other kinds of life. Maybe he knew one parent
could not keep up with three mouths so he flew off to
continue his life, maybe alone, maybe finding a new mate.
Either way, I will miss Momma and the promise of the two
young owls.

We asked ourselves what to do with Momma, and
decided to let her hang there, feathers ruffled by the
strengthening breeze. I marveled at the small but scimitar
like claws, now free of the death grip they had inflicted
on smaller creatures. I wanted to take a long wing or tail
feather, maybe even a foot with the curved talons. This
body was the perfection of creation for predatory birds,
but it didn't belong to me and was not mine to take. I
will never again see this silent but deadly hunter flying
between the trees. Let nature take care of her now. I will
come back later in the year to make sure nothing remains
of the death struggle in this perennial nest. Maybe Papa
will return next year with a new bride. Maybe a new pair
will find and use it; life will continue. This is a perfect
spot for a nest, with abundant food and cover nearby.
Rabbits and chipmunks will breathe free for a while, but
fear will always surround their lives. I might hear the
lonely, heartbreaking hooting of a grieving male owl.
Or maybe not. But I know the night sky will be a more
lonesome place, missing something so deep I cannot fully
understand it.

By late afternoon, an approaching storm replaced

the sunny spring sky with dark and ominous clouds. The
wind was blowing the branches of the nest tree, now just
like others in a forest of green. Feathers of the dead owl
fluttered in the wind. I left, knowing I couldn't go back.
I would avoid the nest tree, casting my attention to new
life coming into bloom. The next day, I welcomed the
hummingbirds, returning from their winter vacation, on
schedule like swallows to Capistrano. I thrilled at the sight
of the lazuli bunting, bringing spring happiness on his blue
and white shoulders. I sat in the sun of another promising
spring day and played an elegy on my cedar flute in the
honor of three feathered bodies. But as with any funeral,
the sadness had to be replaced by the hope and the future.
Three lives were gone, but more would come. Life followed
death and death followed life in that never ending cycle. I
needed to focus on life.

Interlude: Ending As Beginning

The great mystery awaits us all
In emotions from fear to anticipation.
Mostly fear of the unknown,
Mostly anticipation of a beginning.

We mourn when endings come too soon,
The sadness of what could have been.
Sometimes we celebrate and rejoice the complete life,
Although happiness comes hard.

We should be envious,
The possibilities are often unseen,
Lost in grief and tears.
But in any life, birth and death are one in the same.

One must die in order to be born.
Life is a cycle, turning with the seasons.
Opposites in balance.
Good with bad, up with down, yin and yang.

We watch others die, but never ourselves.
We feel not its silent grasp,
Coming seen or unseen, we never feel the crossing.
Suddenly, we walk into the light.

Blinking like a lost bird,
We hesitate, look around, take that first step.
The moment of death is the same moment of birth.
Into what is still that mystery.

The freedom of thought to believe what we wish,
Not restrained by the shackles of religious dogma,
Is the permission to float to the stars.
None of us know the true answer.

Whatever we wish heaven to be, it is.
There is no hell, only for those still living.
Walking through that door is the acceptance
Of the opportunities of the universe.

We join the stars
In their vast cycle of the universe of universes.
Time knows no end or beginning.
Space is as limitless as our imaginations.

Going Home in Time

Backward, turn backward,
Oh time in your flight.
Make me a child again,
Just for tonight.

Elizabeth Akers Allen, "Rock Me to Sleep,"
Yale Book of American Verse

———————————

Time does not become sacred
Until we have lived it.

John Burroughs, "Spell of the Past,"
Writings of John Burroughs

The Last Passenger Pigeon

How did it feel to be the last passenger pigeon? The last one of an entire race to fly free over the skies of the continent, alone, in search of its own kind—friend or family. Did it know it was the last one, never again to see another of its kind in this world?

I can imagine my reactions if I were in its place, although I doubt the bird was thinking those philosophical questions. It was looking for food, searching for a mate, wary of predators. And it died, its kind never to be seen again under this sun and this moon.

These thoughts occurred to me as I sit here looking at a photograph in the family album. It was taken nearly twenty years ago. My father is standing with Tonic, Jug, and Buck—his brothers, also known by their christened names—Clyde, Frank, and Fred. The occasion was a dinner in honor of the four brothers, all of whom had achieved fifty year membership in the Masonic Order. This may have been a record worthy of higher notation, but I don't know if anyone bothered researching it. It didn't receive much publicity since the lodge was in the small community of Mason, Illinois. Pure coincidence, the name. But I think that is what should have caused it to make

national news as one of those cheery little fillers which end
Friday newscasts on happy notes. There can be something
nice in this violent world after all.

It may not be important to many others, but this
photograph and the story behind it have meaning to me.
Mason, Illinois, really doesn't exist anymore. It is one of
those small farming towns that helped build America, but
has since been all but abandoned as so-called progress
moved on. It was the nearest town to where all the brothers
grew up on a farm that doesn't exist anymore either.

My dad's old home place is gone. I never knew it, nor did
I know my grandparents. Their adventures were over before
mine began. I don't even know if the farm survived after
them. I do know it isn't there now, long ago torn down and
disappeared in corn fields, oak thickets, maybe even some
remnants of an Illinois prairie lost even to my grandfather.

Mason is a few old houses and brick buildings, not a
town as we think of it today. I don't even know for sure,
since I've only been there once that I remember. My
grandparents are buried in the small cemetery. Or is it in
Edgewood another mile or two down the road? I really
should know more about these things. The Interstate
passes Mason by. The travelers from Chicago to Memphis
don't even notice this place where the prairies of the north
start mixing with the woodlands of the south. Illinois,
home to Chicago and Abe Lincoln, what else is there to
know? A few thousand years ago, the passenger pigeons
flew here but no further north. The glacier stopped just
about here. Right where an old farmhouse with a family of
thirteen children was sitting about a hundred years ago.

But more important than the farm, or the town, is the
fact that the brothers are gone now, too. All but one. They
all lived into their nineties. They grew up on the Illinois

prairie soil; they were as tough as the sod and oak thickets that once fed the masses of passenger pigeons. Thirteen children—only one of the boys remains. Just like the last passenger pigeon, he once flew with the rest of the flock. He is now the last. How does it feel? The bird may not have felt emotions. People do.

Ninety summers of August sun. I go back in my imagination to a day when the air is steamy and the horizon dimmed by the haze. Yesterday's thunderstorm left the bottomland soil of reddish yellow clay a gumbo down by the riverbank. The boys don't dare go down there fishing today. Mom will tan their hides if they track that sticky mud into the kitchen. The railroad tracks that pass close to the farm form a double line fading into the horizon, not far off. I can hear the lonely wail signaling the disappearance of the daily doodle bug. It was not the main line of the B&O or the C&EI or the Illinois Central, but just a small side line. The girls are giggling as they hang up the laundry on the one wire line out back. Maybe they think the holes in the boy's underwear are funny.

But now, as I return to the present in my mind, there is only silence. Except for the crickets. Somehow, they make the heat even more oppressive. The boredom of one corn field stretching into another is oppressive to me. Where is the diversity and excitement that once lingered on this now bare October field?

Most of the brothers greeted the twentieth century, back in the days when memories still lingered of old Abe from Springfield, not that far down the road. It was in a time when the old men still sat around the general store in Mason or Edgewood and retold stories of the Civil War. And possibly even stories of shooting passenger pigeons, and wolves, and buffalo "out west".

Ninety winters of January blizzards passed by with weeks on end of a steel gray sky, no trace of a sun overhead. Freezing rain turned to snow, then the north wind piled up drifts covering the tracks. "Keep the turkeys off the tracks" were the daily orders. There were no school buses then. The line of the doodle bug was the only plowed trail. The walk to town was nearly a killer more than once. The bobwhite quail hunkered down in the snowdrifts under the thickets.

The last passenger pigeon hunkered down by himself (or was it herself? It had a name) and died alone in the Cincinnati Zoo. I should know this. We all should. The particular bird survived much less than ninety summers and winters. But its kind survived ninety times ninety centuries throwing shadows that lasted for hours on end over the Illinois prairie and bottomland. We should include in our daily prayers a request for forgiveness for what we did. Extinction is forever. The bird was a creation of our God, and we destroyed it by our ignorance and arrogance.

Ecclesiastes wisely states that men may come and men may go, but earth abides. Pigeons come and go, as do grizzlies and buffalo. Farms and towns come and they go. Families do too, mothers and fathers, brothers and sisters. But the people have memories, not so with buildings and railroad tracks. Pigeons may not remember, but they have built-in memories called instinct. The millennia of memories that were part of every pigeon are gone. What secrets died with the last bird?

I look again at the photo. Four brothers shared the secrets of an ancient order, as well as the secrets of a now abandoned farm, along with the family that lived there. Secrets that are disappearing along with the passenger pigeons long decayed in the black prairie soil. Listen to the names. Jug, Tonic, Buck. It may have been hard to name thirteen kids. They must have thought their given names boring. They all had nicknames that are a story in themselves. My Dad's given name was Raleigh. The story was that his parents didn't name him right away, but waited a few days or weeks. He had a rash that Raleigh ointment cured. So they named him after that ointment. Of course that name didn't take, so his brothers called him Bob. Not as in short for Robert, but because when he followed his older siblings, he bobbed along behind them. He was known as Bob, or even Raleigh Bob. All his siblings had similar stories. I never knew why my uncles had names like Tonic or Jug or Buck or why my aunts had names like BeeWee and Bing. I only have one brother, so I will never know what it was like to come from a large family.

Did the pigeons mate for life? I don't know that, but I do know that my father did. For over fifty years. She is not in the photo, but she is just out of the picture. She was by his side for over half a century and was the only one I know who ever called him Raleigh. She is gone now too. So the loneliness increases with the disappearance of most people and things that shared those ninety springs and Indian summers. I cannot ask him about that. Some things are too personal.

Pigeons had no memories, no emotions as we recognize to pass on to their young. They lived as part of their world and they disappeared, as individuals and as a species. We live and disappear as individuals. The species continues on. But as the old farms decay into the prairie soil, the small towns disappear into memories. The photographs become memories of times forever gone. I wonder if the species is still the same. It is a different world. A world without passenger pigeons is a lonelier world. A world without the small towns is, too.

I cannot count ninety summers yet; I now count just over fifty. Will the memories fade? Do they start to blur together? I look into the smiles in the photographs. There were four. Now there is one. Did they see any pigeons? Do the three see any now? Is that what the smiles are about? I cannot know. I cannot know what the last passenger pigeon would have thought if he could think. Maybe when you are the last one, the memories are not important. Maybe you just think of the fact you are still there. And you dream of darkened skies as you soar with your brothers and sisters. And a boyhood home with October skies and April rains that will stretch forever with no worry of ever ending.

I wonder. I set the photo down and turn the page of the photo album. I look now at a photo of me and my brother. We are young and we are smiling.

I wrote this in 1995. My father passed away in 2002, age 96. Now there are none.

ROUTE 36

Katherine and I were sitting at the edge of US Highway 36, east of Smith Center, Kansas in 2001, reading the sign that proclaimed this, or more accurately a spot only four miles away, as the exact geographic center of the contiguous United States. We were on our way to Tuscola to visit my dad for a short vacation. He was well into his nineties and we knew there would not be very many more trips across the plains, trips that I had taken many times the past thirty-six years.

It was a sunny April afternoon with a cool breeze waving the new growth of lime-green grass and the still leafless tree branches. The west breeze was pushing the dying remnants of a vicious spring snowstorm to a safe distance north and east of us, a storm that put us here rather than much further east on Interstate 70. We struggled all afternoon the previous day to get out of Colorado, but the wake of this fast moving blizzard left all routes east of Denver closed and us defeated in our efforts to flank the storm and break past it. Spring blizzards on the high plains have a way of humbling anything and everything that moves. I had been caught before in these storms. At least we were not caught in this one, just behind it. It still played havoc with our travel.

So we ended up a day later than expected, but on our way east again and on an old friend. An old friend that I had only visited in bits and pieces in the last thirty-six years—U.S. Highway 36 in Kansas. This highway was

special to me since it formed the southern edge of my
hometown in Illinois. It guided the west wind into and out
of town and was the path that led to places far away and
unknown to a small town boy. It was an important east-
west route before the impersonal Interstate 70 replaced it
as a major high speed route.

I first noticed a trace of the original highway west
of Smith Center. It was a few yards south of the current
highway and now a part of the wide grassy right of way,
but was basically intact. What used to be a bumpy, narrow,
concrete surface that supported millions of passing tires,
was now a peaceful grassy strip, recognizable only by eyes
at least fifty years old and in search of memories. Rather
than widening the old highway, engineers sometime in the
past decades simply abandoned the old surface and moved
over a hundred yards to build a new highway. The pioneer
spirit still lived on. Why recycle when there is new country
to use up?

It was memory that blew in the breeze as I walked
down that wide flat path, with dog Varda in tow. Few
vehicles passed by on the modern highway of this new
century as I wandered east for a few dozen yards from
the rest area. I felt the wind blow years from my mind as
easily as it waved the grass.

It was 1955, or maybe 1957; I didn't remember for
sure. Accuracy and memory are not always a compatible
couple. It didn't matter. I was with my mother, passengers
with my Uncle Chuck as he drove from Illinois to his new
home in Boulder, Colorado. He had returned to Illinois for
some reason now known only to the wind; we were riding
with him back to his new home in Boulder. My mom and I
would later take the train back to our own home.

This was world class excitement for me. Colorado.

The mountains. The myth and mystery of exotic places. I yearned, at about this spot, to see the mountains. Of course this was one of a long string of life's major disappointments; it would be another half day before we came close enough to finally see those small purple lumps capped by white dots that became the Front Range and not just another cloud touching the horizon. I remember that magic place, that hole in the road on Route 36 called Joes, Colorado, where I got my first glance. That may still have been wishful thinking, but the air was clearer and cleaner back in '55, or was it '57? Maybe it really was that far east where we first glimpsed those purple peaks. I do remember we stayed at a motel in Smith Center, forcing me to wait another day before I saw those magic mountains.

And they were magic. I fell in love with the Rocky Mountains. And with Boulder and the Flatirons and the house of my Uncle Chuck and Aunt Mabel on Gilbert Street at the base of Flagstaff Mountain. The mountains and the West proved to be my destiny. From that time on, I was tugged like iron to a magnet by Colorado and the mountains. I was never the same after that. That trip on that old highway, U.S. 36, was my rebirth, though a few years premature.

Several times I returned to Boulder, always via U.S. Highway 36. Interstate 70 did not then exist. I have since returned many times via I-70 from Colorado and points west to the old Illinois home. When not in a hurry, I often turned off I-70 to follow lesser roads that peacefully wind and wend through a slower, quieter farmland. Roads that allow a traveler to see the real towns, the stately courthouses in the center of town, the tree-lined brick streets and Victorian homes with bicycles in the yard and neighbors swapping gossip over the back fence, if there is a back fence. Small town Kansas or Missouri life still exists, refugee from the I-70 pace that blurs one town from another, one Wal-Mart from the next.

The last time I traveled the full length of US 36 from Tuscola to Boulder was in June,1965. That trip was as magical as my first but for a different reason. I had just graduated from high school and classmate Tim Lemna and I headed west from Tuscola on a journey of celebration and freedom. I'm sure we pulled off in his 1944 black Ford at this same rest area at the center of the known universe and counted the miles to our dreams on a late June afternoon. That trip, over new territory for Tim but familiar for me, was an end of one freedom of childhood and the beginning of another one out West. We were both soon to be on our own and this route, by now a familiar face to me, was a comforting transition from old to new. I was to leave Tuscola for good and start college in Idaho in a couple months. That June journey was a preview trip

Blinking back to the year 2001, I watched Varda as she stood motionless, nose in the air, inhaling the breeze that brought no memories to her, only a symphony of smells. Her eyes closed and nose twitching, she was reading more than history. She was transcending time, as I wished I could do. I longed to go beyond 1955, or '57. Far beyond. I longed for a swath of grassy prairie that hid not an old highway, but a trail of Kiowa or Arapaho, a mastodon and hint of a not so far off glacier, still lurking to the north.

But I knew I would have to settle for a highway I dreamed of yearly in those years of the mid 50s, starting about this time of year. I dreamed of traveling in July or August, on that odyssey west to Boulder or points beyond. I remember the narrow road as a roller coaster of concrete up a hill and down the swale, cornfield and fencerows crowding the edge of the pavement. A pavement with upturned edges, almost like a long curb stretching across the prairie. There were still Burma Shave signs and smaller homemade billboards announcing small motels and restaurants. Businesses which later disappeared with the retirement of their owners as traffic on U.S. 36 moved south to the new and faster Interstate 70. There were small farms, with houses and barns hugging the road and old half rotten fence posts lining the narrow right of way. These barns were crumbling now, with the old two-story houses replaced by sprawling ranch style homes set farther back off the highway.

And I remembered the cemeteries. Sweet Home, Mt. Hope, St. Elizabeth, Lutheran. All with the wrought iron arched gate, in imitation and expectation of the ultimate Pearly Gate. The final resting place, or more properly waiting place, for the pioneers and the sons and daughters of those hardy settlers of the wilderness of grass of over a hundred years ago. The signs at the cemetery proclaimed the location of the churches, just down the road a piece. They were the center for the community defining the people and who they were. Unlike the Pawnee or Arapaho, whose only community was the expanse of grass from horizon to horizon and beyond. Their homes went with them and the definition of who they were was the expanse of grass itself. And the buffalo. The limitless herds were the first to go, with the Pawnee and Arapaho soon to disappear as well. Now the pioneers were disappearing too. Soon only the west wind would remain, that tireless and never ending zephyr bringing promises of a still golden west.

I walked back to the car, sitting next to that sign showing mileages from this center of the known world to everywhere else. Over 500 miles to anywhere. We had a

long way to go and I realized that mileages meant nothing.
I had come a long way from that first trip in 1955 or '57.
I had crossed this vast prairie on a ribbon of cracked
concrete. I had crossed it many times. Each direction
carried me home. One home was where I grew up; one
home was beyond the far off mountains where I longed
to roam. One home on the flat fertile shore where glaciers
deposited their load, one on the high uplifted shore where
mountain glaciers began up close to the clouds.

We got in the car and pulled back onto the modern
highway. We said goodbye to the small shaded rest area
and soon said goodbye to the old highway as the flat
grassy surface faded away, old concrete culverts no longer
marking the trail. The last evidence I saw of old 36 was
the bridge over the Republican River near Scandia. It was
the original narrow bridge, lined by crumbling concrete
pillared edges. A thought crossed my mind of an analogy
of the old moderate Republican Party of my youth and
the old Republican River bridge, both now falling apart,
but I let that slide by, as the grand old river slid by below,
disappearing in the muddy oak and willow thickets.

Just before that bridge, we passed a funeral caravan
heading west. I thought about turning around and joining
it in tribute, but we were already a half day late. And
maybe this trip was not the one for me to stand silent as
some stranger, probably a grandson of a pioneer settler
long turned to dust, was laid to rest in Mount Hope
Cemetery, to await that day when he could look up and
see an unbroken expanse of prairie, grass waving from
horizon to horizon in a spring breeze just like today. Where
a mastodon was standing at the southern edge of that
great northern glacier. A day when promise and hope was
as fresh as the spring beauties now lining the highway in

those few undisturbed patches of forest.

I had a long way to go, as had we all. The route was old, yet the highway was young. Spring was coming on fast now, and soon the leaves would shade another car sitting by that sign proclaiming the center of the world. And as the big bluestem reached for the sky, awaiting the passing thunder of the buffalo, maybe some young boy would stop here. A youth on his first trip from that eastern shore of this ocean of waving prairie grass to the mystic Rocky Mountains of his dreams, sitting on the western shore of the endless prairie. I whispered to his listening ears. Enjoy it all now and remember it well. Places that proclaim to be the center of the known world tend to become sacred. They take on meanings that require thousands of miles of travel on unknown pathways. They require thousands of sunrises to witness the journeys and discoveries that make it sacred. The zephyr breeze of understanding only comes once as it passes over the far off glacier on its way south to meet the waving ocean of prairie grass.

Homebound on the Zephyr

Amtrak's famed California Zephyr snaked through a remote steep walled gorge of the Colorado River west of Kremmling, Colorado, in April 2002. Looking out the observation car window, my eyes followed the winding path of an old abandoned trail on the hillside across the river. It disappeared under a rockslide, then reappeared on the other side. It had probably been decades since anyone trod that lonely path. Once, some optimistic prospector led his mule along the trail, watching nothing but his burro's footprints in a desolate canyon. Then as progress came to the mountains, he observed the construction of a life-changing railroad and soon the afternoon freight that slowly passed by. The future lay not on his side of the canyon, but on the other side as that daily freight and passenger train would bring settlement to this wild mountain land. It would not carry his fortune in gold. His fortune passed him by, just as my train was passing by his memory. No one now remembered his name. Gold in these hills faded into dreams as now did the snow, rapidly melting under the April sun. There was never any road built through this gorge. Only the railroad tracks and the traces of a long lost footpath on the other side of the canyon allowed people to see the rocky splendor of this unknown section of a famous and scenic river.

Reentering civilization after leaving the remote canyon, the train crept into Kremmling, then approached the condos and trophy homes of Winter Park. The light of the sinking sun faded as the train entered the famous Moffat tunnel and soon descended jerkily down the mountain in the snowy darkness. Lights of the Front Range mega city beckoned and teased us for miles down the slow descent into the maze of rail yards on the edge of downtown Denver.

As we slowly maneuvered through the yards, I thought back nearly fifty years. My mother and I got on this very same California Zephyr in Denver one summer day back in the mid '50s. We had earlier driven to Boulder with Uncle Chuck from his old home in Champaign to his new home in the quiet town with the famous Flatirons. Mom and I were returning to Illinois via the train. My only vivid memory of the trip was the tremendous earache I had by the time we got to Chicago which kept me from enjoying the Field Museum as we waited to change trains for the final leg south to home.

The jostling of the train as it eased into Union Station in Denver brought me back to the present. This train and this trip were carrying me back in time. It, and possibly I as well, were becoming an anachronism for 21st century America. I thought about this a lot the next day as the magnificent mountain scenery of Colorado changed into rolling farmlands of Nebraska and Iowa. As I watched the green fields pass by silently on a cool but sunny spring day, it dawned on me that this trip was my last look at a distant past. I was going home for the final time. I buried my 96-year-old father a few weeks before and now I was going home to close up the house and sell it. Home, where I grew up on the flat Illinois prairie, would no longer be a home I could ever return to again. My parents had bought this house in 1934 when they were married and it was the home I grew up in. It now sat hauntingly empty yet full of furniture, stuff, and memories. Not for much longer, I thought, as I watched farm fields pass in silent apathy.

But how do you close down and sell a house that holds over a half century worth of memories? How do you come home for the last time, knowing you will never come home again? In my mind and my memory, the old house and small town would of course forever be home, but now I had no more living ties to it. It was a past without a future. As I watched the scenery flash silently by, I felt the pull of a past no longer there outside mere thoughts in my mind. The California Zephyr itself was a past and a memory still barely holding on.

The California Zephyr. The name itself was enough to bring images of something golden, promised, but totally unknown to a small boy from rural Illinois. A zephyr was a gentle west wind. A breeze coming from the golden land of California and the Colorado Rockies brought promises and the lure of magic. It was now taking me home to the past.

I went down to the lounge car and bought a sandwich for lunch. I wanted to sit quietly and watch the fields roll by. I noticed they were selling souvenirs in addition to food. My eyes focused on a deck of playing cards. A picture of an Amtrak train crossing Donner Pass with Donner Lake below it made me think of another deck of cards somewhere in a desk back in that home in Illinois. My mom took my older brother to California to visit an aunt and uncle the Christmas when I was only three years old. I was left with my dad, who in turn left me with a friend to babysit me. I guess his idea of a couple weeks of bachelorhood didn't include working all day, then coming home to tend me. I have no memory of the whole thing, but I do remember the deck of cards with the logo and words California Zephyr in faded mauve colors. We played canasta often with those cards. Never again would my

parents and my brother pull out the card table, pop some
popcorn, shuffle the deck and laugh about Uncle Bee
cheating the last time we played him. I had to buy this new
deck of cards to complete the history of that famous train
in my life. One deck signified my youth, the second my
maturity. I would never play canasta with this deck, but
I needed it to complete a cycle. Or maybe to complete a
circle that would be forever broken. Going home to a past I
was holding onto.

I watched as the train passed scenery that itself was just
holding on. Leaning and broken phone lines, abandoned
now to the pull of gravity, still lined the tracks, obviously
forgotten and ignored by even insulator collectors. Old
brick buildings and warehouses sat vacant with windows
broken out and roofs caving in. We didn't pass by the new
malls and housing developments lining the freeways. The
rail lines passed through the decay of a time past. A past
that was all I had left of a place I forever called home. These
buildings, once the pride of a nation, now sat abandoned,
forgotten, unloved. The For Rent signs competed with signs
announcing rewards for information about anyone breaking
windows. One last hope for renewal, this wishful optimism.

I had winced when we pulled into Omaha a few miles
back. Old brick warehouses were falling down. Windows
were boarded up. Magnificent old stations, once works
of art and the centerpiece of their towns, were now
abandoned and deemed safety hazards. Cities took pride
in saving historic old buildings in rotting downtowns and
riverfronts. Why did they turn their backs on the work
places and warehouses that fueled the growth of the cities
in their periods of youth?

An overwhelming sense of anachronism rushed over
me as I rolled through the greening of the winter wheat

fields of southern Iowa. An anachronism of not only the railroad, but the small towns and vacant buildings as well. Rumors were once again in the news of the demise of Amtrak. These rumors had surfaced and subsided in the past years as common as April robins pecking through the brown winter grass.

The once magnificent and powerful railroads signified an era fading into the past. Once you could travel wherever you wished via railroad. I remember hopping on the City of New Orleans with my third grade class for a quick trip from Champaign to Chicago. It was a learning experience. Up and back in one long day for patient railroad conductors and screaming school kids. I cherish an old black and white photo of me smiling at the camera in my mother's hands, while I was holding hands with my neighbor and best friend, Jimmy Allison. Meanwhile, our distracted teacher, Mrs. Bundy looks as if she was searching for a way out of that chaos.

The railroads built this country, especially the West. Railroads in the East simply connected already existing towns and villages. Trains brought the settlers to the plains of the West as this growing country slowly inched its way through the zephyr winds to the golden land of the Pacific Coast. Then the tide of people blew towards California and the new dream. Towns survived or disappeared based on whether the railroad chose to come or chose to stay. The railroads burrowed into hidden valleys of the Rockies in search of gold. They carried the results of our factories to small towns everywhere. They moved the grain and food the settlers produced. They displaced a culture and civilization we stubbornly and manifestly refused to accept.

Now our factories sat decayed and empty, as did so many of the small towns. I realized we didn't produce anything now. We serviced and we computed. We drove and flew everywhere. But we did not ride the train.

I watched the Iowa scenery change to even flatter Illinois scenery as we crossed the Father of Rivers. Looking around the nearly empty lounge car, I wondered why it wasn't full of travelers like me.

But then I really didn't want to see travelers like me. That would be too sad. I was making one last trip to a home that soon wouldn't exist any longer. I felt like the countryside I was passing through soon would not exist either. Small family farms interspersed with the factories and business of the cities were going the way of the railroad. They were intertwined. One needed the other. When one disappeared, the other had to be close behind.

The lonely wail of the train horn echoed past the rolling fields and empty sidings of old elevators. One last trip through an America that was changing from my past. Progress always had a price and my values might not be the values of the next generation. Just as I missed out on the horse and buggy, the child born today may miss out on the excitement of taking a cross country trip on the California Zephyr. It would be a loss for both of us.

As we pulled into Chicago and Union Station, I prepared to leave the California Zephyr and climb aboard the City of New Orleans for the last leg of my nostalgic journey. The City of New Orleans brought even more personal memories. That was the train that daily screamed past the edge of my small home town. Chicago to New Orleans. I remembered playing Little League baseball in Ervin Park. We could set our watches, usually in about the fifth inning, to the regular 8 o'clock City of New Orleans, southbound from Chicago, fresh out of the station in Champaign. It traveled between magical cities

in a world I didn't know, but spoke of exciting things. I
started humming the song by Arlo Guthrie. It sang of the
heartland, the steady presence through time, something
we could count on forever.

I could count on it forever. I could hear the laughter
and screams of excited third graders. They all echoed in
my memory, along with the wail of the steam locomotives
winding through the Colorado Rockies. Home, one last
time on a gentle breeze.

THE COON TREE

It stands in silent watch beside the river. It is an ancient and massive oak, but any name spoken in less than a thousand words cannot describe this living sculpture of bark and moss. It has seen a hundred floods of spring and a hundred painted autumns filled with scrambling squirrels and silent deer. It sits in a hollow by the river, left untouched by five generations of anxious but humble farmers. Long ago, the rest of the forest was cleared and burned, the smoke choking the sapling oak. For years, the steady plod of the mule and creak of harness leather meant the smell of musty black earth. One spring the mule came no more—replaced by a coughing and sputtering John Deere, and the smell of diesel. The battles with floodwater and thistle have ended for now; for the past two seasons, the field has stood quiet, unbroken but for the woodchuck holes. The air vibrates only to the quail and woodpecker, echoing forever down the river.

You can't see it from this side, but the hole is up there below the dead limb. It has been home to dozens of generations of raccoons. Masked balls of fur clambering up and down every branch, just to test the will of poor old mom. Possums used it too, waiting in turn with the great horned owl, and even one spring, the wood ducks. There was almost always a big squirrel nest wadded between the limbs way up on top. The tree has provided shelter and supper to untold hundreds of creatures feathered and furred.

The old coon hunters were by here last week, but they don't come around much anymore. They're getting tired, like the tree. And besides, their old blue hound died a few years back. You could hear him bellowing a mile away, with the flashlights following him far behind, swinging up and down, stumbling in the old ditch just past the fence.

No coon climbed the tree this year. The old dead limb fell to the ground during a storm last July and the bottom branch finally died. There must be ten pounds of buckshot in those branches, but the bark has quietly and gently embedded them safely away. The old tree has given life to many, but it is also the tombstone for several more. It is quietly joining them now, becoming its own epitaph. It won't see many more blizzards, but then, who will notice? A tall young sapling is already up to the level of the den hole. And that hickory had its first crop of nuts this year.

The night sky is bitter cold, but sparkling clear. The broken and gnarled branches reach up towards the full moon, casting a thousand shadows on the frozen snow. I stand here in the moonlight and close my eyes. I can hear the slow steady plod of the mule up there in the field, and a distant voice calling out something about lemonade being ready for lunch. And I can feel the autumn wind send the brown and gold leaves twisting, twirling, falling to the water below. And the strange and haunting music of that old coon dog echoing through the night.

My roots reach into this black soil as surely as those of this tree. The coons and the quail will always be here. So will I and so will the tree.

Granddad's Barn

I never knew my granddad. He left this earth long before I was able to watch him whittle a piece of hickory branch, or ask him questions about the way he would hitch up a team of mules, or to listen to him tell stories of what it was like growing up in Tennessee decades before. His life was always hard, but life usually was hard for people like him. He was a farmer but without his own land. He had raised my mom and her four sisters and one brother in a house on the edge of town. The house, the family, the evidence of there ever being a Granddad Hance was history by the time I was old enough to remember any of it. But there was a barn, standing alone in a field several miles west of town. I can remember many times driving by that barn and listening to my mom say that was Dad's barn.

The barn is gone now, as are most of Granddad's children. It rests now in the memory of my mind, no longer on the black soil of the Illinois prairie. Its ashes are now part of the soil itself, giving new life to cornstalks and ragweed and fireflies on sultry August evenings.

I cannot identify the field where the barn once stood. It merges with thousands of other similar fields now in an expanse of boredom on this flat prairie land. I pick a field at random and pretend it is the one where the barn stood. I close my eyes and in my mind join my mother and watch her gaze across the plowed field. We see nothing but the stillness of another time. No hedgerows to shelter the pheasant. Not even the broken cornstalks yielding a hidden treasure to feed the hogs sent into the field on a November afternoon. Only the lazy puffs of summer clouds break the stillness, painting in my mind a vision of a day long ago.

I see the gray and weathered boards and rusted pieces of wire framing the barn. The vines struggle to climb the walls, the burs secretly position themselves to attack bare feet. The old black Ford sits next to the barn waiting as patiently as the old mule used to. There is no horizon, just neighboring fields as square as a quilt thrown over the countryside.

Swallows circle the building claiming sanctuary from the crows over in the trees, just down the road a piece. The cicadas sing their song and a lonely frog peeps mournfully somewhere by the ditch. The old red pump, with its rusted and worn handle drips onto the moist dirt. It echoes the screech of the metal as the pump handle falls out of Granddad's hand. The splash of water quickly fades into the green sea of corn as he wipes his face, red from the sun and heat, with his old torn bandana.

I can smell the black soil and the mustiness of the barn. The heat of this summer day lies on the field like a blanket of steam. It doesn't bother Granddad. He fingers his hat as he stares past the barn, neither his eyes nor his mind see anything in that field. Only he knows what memory has just passed by in the shadow of the hawk. Maybe another August day back in '98. Or another barn or maybe a Tennessee road winding through the woods. Another age, as lost to him as his is to me this summer evening.

He knows every inch of the barn. Exactly where he put that piece of rope that was always six inches too short. The corner of the loft where he bumped into the bat that October evening. The crack in the floor where he lost his favorite screwdriver. The corner post he always intended to fix. How many times did he nudge it with the wagon?

The old barn withstood thunderstorms and blizzards, stoically ignoring one crisis after another. Another pair of shoes to buy, another year with the same worn-out plow. The price of corn was always a disappointment. Hogs usually did well, but chickens were a bother.

I look down as a water drop falls from the sea blue cloudless sky. I look up and the barn is gone. So is Mom and so is Granddad. He was here, with the barn and a pump and a rusted screwdriver lying in a pile of soil and ash. A way of life was here and is no more. And the clouds drift out of the west on that old familiar zephyr breeze, following the hawks and fireflies. Change, constant change that is shuffling, erasing, and reshuffling life is on that breeze. The swallows come with the breeze, passing in apathy over a freshly plowed field while a memory changes a tear to a smile.

Interlude: Little Boy Blue

The house was now empty.
Memories reflected off the walls.
Seventy long years after a newlywed couple started their life.
My task now was to say goodbye and walk away.

I grew up and they grew old.
It was home and forever will be.
But from now on, it would live only in memories.
I had to clean, sort, and pack the stuff of those lives.

Some things I had never seen,
Some were old friends long hidden.
I was a peeping Tom of personal secrets,
None of them mine, but now all I had left of parents both gone.

In the bottom of the bedroom cedar chest,
I found the treasure. A school project of my mother.
Unseen for well over half a century at least, never by me.
It was her secret of a youth lost in a world long passed.

Little Boy Blue, the poem by Eugene Field.
Copied carefully in her own hand.
Next to a magazine picture of the toys.
A little tin soldier, a sad eyed bear, a dusty attic chair.

A small A+ down in the corner, by her name.
Given by a teacher long forgotten.
A small rip in the corner of the poster board.
Two paper clipped strips of ribbon, purple and blue.
Nothing else.

The little toy dog is covered with dust,
But sturdy and stanch he stands,
And the little toy soldier is red with rust,
And his musket moulds in his hands.

Lost in the emotions of the task, laying to rest two lives,
I read the poem, thought of the pride of my mother
Finishing this project as a little girl.
Maybe a teardrop, a soft sigh as she thought of her life ahead.

Time was when the little toy dog was new,
And the soldier was passing fair.
And that was the time when Little Boy Blue
Kissed them and put them there.

More than a tear for me.
I lost it as all the emotion and grief came to the moment.
I was seeing a glimpse of a mother I never knew: a schoolgirl.
Her life ahead of her, unknown. Not a hint of my time to come.

Now don't you go til I come, he said,
And don't you make any noise,
So toddling off to his trundle bed,
He dreamt of the pretty toys.

"Little Boy Blue" of the poem abandons his youth by death,
Leaving the toys to dust and rust.
My thoughts were less sad, but maybe not.
Toys and youth abandoned to time. The effect the same.

And as he was dreaming, an angel song
Awakened our Little Boy Blue.
Oh! the years are many, the years are long,
But the little toy friends are true.

The loss of youth. The little soldier rusting and broken.
The doll not needed as youth grows.
Did she guess the significance of the poem?
We lose childhood friends along with their innocence.

"Puff the Magic Dragon" mourned the same idea,
We leave our friends of youth.
Time rushes by.
Much too soon, time is all we have.

I became lost in my youth, my life, my grief.
Not knowing her childhood, half of her life, her sorrows.
What toys did she abandon? What hopes did she dream
As she read the poem of sadness.

Ay, faithful to Little Boy Blue they stand,
Each in the same old place,
Awaiting the touch of a little hand,
The smile of a little face.

I had never thought of her as a girl.
Mothers restart their lives with their first child.
And they are always there,
For their little boys with their own toy soldiers.

For a lifetime, until they are gone. Forever.
Then we realize, we understand, we grieve.
Too late to say I care, I want to know.
When did you say goodbye to your little boy blue?

And they wonder as waiting the long years through,
In the dust of that little chair,
What has become of our Little Boy Blue,
Since he kissed them and put them there?

You saved the poem, the picture.
What did it mean to you? Did you ever think back?
Of course you did. We all do. Don't we?
When do we stop growing up?

I never made my own poster,
Printed in my own hand.
I wished I did. Maybe I could make one now.
No, I will keep my Mother's. I think she would like that.

She is smiling now, sitting by her own dusty chair.
She will understand my tears. I can feel her hand on
      my shoulder.
Like she always did when I was sad.
Some things you never forget.

You may outgrow the toy soldiers,
The stuffed bears, the little boy blues.
A mother's comfort and childhood friends.
But the memories only grow stronger.

I cradled the poster, carefully packed it for its final journey.
It sits now hidden in my own chest.
I cannot look at it now. The tears blur the words.
I look forward to talking to her about it. Someday,
      I can then ask,

What has become of little girl blue,
Since she kissed them and put them there?

Interlude: The Pictures

Carol sent me a time machine.
Pictures rescued from a dusty shelf
One class out of four
For the future Class of '65.

Go back to a day of our youth,
May 21, 1957.
Springtime meant an ending.
Schools out, time to play.

South Ward, a week before they became 5th graders.
First the boys lined up,
Then a picture of the girls.
Why divide that way? Old habits die hard.

Look at the faces.
Do you remember them?
They became us, they portend their own future.
Did they have any idea then?

I want to talk to them
To ask if they have any idea.
We know now how it turns out.
Their innocent faces look into a camera that became
     the future.

The handwritten captions are simple:
Girls of the 4th Grade,
Boys of the 4th Grade.
Their attention is a week away.

Why are the boys so dour?
Only one smile, and that a clownish grin.
Larry was happy, but Larry disappeared.
Within 15 years he was lost to all of us.

Were they serious because they knew their future?
Vietnam for some, divorce for others,
Nearly half stayed near home,
Only one remains unidentified.

Who was the mystery boy?
And why don't any of us remember him?
I feel sorry that he left our memories.
Does he remember us?

The girls are happier.
Nine are smiling,
Kathy, arms folded, smiles in mischievous mystery.
What does she know?

Nancy has her hands on Barb's shoulder in a
    protective manner.
Carol holds hands with Mary,
Terry fondly has her arm around Tanya,
Becky's smile mirrors Larry's—a clown grin.

Is their future any brighter?
Tragedy lurks for some.
Fame for others.
Motherhood for most.

I look closely, riveted by memories.
I knew none when the pictures were taken.
But in a few years, we were all together for a brief time.
Faces from the past. Times long gone.

The people are still with us,
Scattered by different lives,
But the moment is gone
When we could stand in front of a blackboard.

It proclaimed a springtime when we were ten.
Strawberries were ripening,
Skies were threatening rain
On a May day long ago.

Few of us remember clearly.
Years are eroding the details,
But the feeling comes back vaguely.
We were young and our future was ahead.

I want to go back and whisper in their ears.
Enjoy it now. Things will change.
Life happens, then it speeds by in a blur.
But I cannot go back. None of us can.

We live life, day by day, always wanting something else.
If we could but trade places with the camera.
Jump ahead a half century, see where it all leads.
But that is the mystery of life.

We all had a dream, a life of fantasy.
A sense of wonder could sustain failures.
We didn't yet even think of our futures.
We were busy growing up.

So Carol and Max, Thank you for the time travel.
We journeyed back to a time of wonder,
Spring days when strawberries and baseball were on
    our minds.
New dresses, new friends next year.

Maybe we still dream,
Of times of youth, times of wonder.
Look into the eyes in the mirror.
They are seeing their future. It is us. It is now. Let us
    smile this time.

THE COSMIC ZEPHYR

Time goes, you say?
Ah no!
Alas, time stays,
We go.

Henry Austin Dobson, "Paradox of Time,"
Works of Henry Austin Dobson

———◆———

Now I have the time.
Where are you?

Rod McKuen, "Another Monday, Two Months Later,"
Valentines

Starry, Starry Skies

One hundred years of life on this planet is a time span beyond the reach of most people. One hundred years ago, it was even more unreachable. Five hundred years before that, it was almost unheard of in common people. In the mind-expanding explosion of technology, the medical achievements we have perfected have increased the potential lifespan of humans. We have done little to tinker with the life spans of most other forms of life, but that has not been our objective. Maybe it should be, since we are causing an amount of worldwide extinctions of species not seen for millions of years.

We are seeing more, understanding more, while also forgetting more of where we really came from. Yet, we continually hear stories of aboriginal peoples living hundreds of years. The shamans, holy people, Tibetan monks, Andean healers, all those so-called primitives who reportedly have that power to see things most of us don't see, few of us hear or feel. Yes, I respond, but they still live as part of nature and do remember where we came from and how we fit in with all other forms of life. We, as a supposedly advanced civilization, have lost that. So, what do we believe?

I can sit under a large juniper tree at the end of the

ridge, looking out over the valley, aglow with the man-made sparkles of car lights, house lights, security outdoor lights spreading photons outward towards space and unknown eyes looking down on us. My location is dark enough that I see the panorama spread out above me, the Milky Way, the entire night sky in its endless glory, the heavens stretching to infinity. Aha. That is the catch: infinity. What does that mean? Could I, or could anyone, even begin to understand what that means? Infinity. Without end. Forever.

My frame of reference is my own life, maybe at some future time reaching that one hundred year mark. Experts say our universe is over fourteen billion years old. We cannot even fathom what happened before that fourteen billion year old beginning. Experts also say that time actually began then. There was nothing, literally nothing before that. I certainly cannot comprehend what that even means. So how many one hundred year spans in just one of those billions? Exactly ten million. Bottom line? We cannot fathom the meaning of our own universe.

The last time I sat on the rim of the Grand Canyon, marveling at the expanse of space and time of the rocks below me, I was as usual astounded at the display of earth history. In that setting, I was looking at a mere few hundred million years of our past. A drop in the bucket as we measure time. In that drop, our planet and its web of life were already old. I could see rocks laid in ancient seas even before dinosaurs ruled all life. Before the beds of peat and decayed trees that turned into coal and oil were laid on ancient swamp floors. Before anything lived on land outside the protective cover of seawater.

Our universe, as we guess it to be, was old before our sun was created. Our telescopes see galaxies billions and billions of years old. And there are billions and billions of galaxies. We have no idea we are even seeing to the edge of the universe, or if it even has one. I lay on a ridge of the uplifted Colorado Rockies, watching falling stars paint the sky, breathing pure air filtered by snow and ice and columbines and pikas, trying to understand the meaning of time. I can see into and past time as it speeds towards me and my home, passing by on an endless journey of infinity. No beginning, no end. I am a small speck of life, living in a speck of time in a forgotten corner of a universe that holds secrets I will never know. Not in a billion years.

A moose could wander by, head down, looking only for a mouthful of willow shoots and not be concerned with what was above her head. An eagle could float on the thermals, higher and higher, enjoying the pure thrill of free flight, and not think about what a billion light years meant. An aspen tree, dropping its golden orbs of leaves in a September breeze, could be said to reach for the stars, but ignorant of anything but the nourishment its roots brought from the soil below. Even my own kind, with its cerebrum of billions of neurons, too often thought only of Friday night football, played under that night sky of infinity, or of a case of Coors, enjoyed around a campfire, spitting photons of light from burning pine branches, onto a journey that could last for fourteen billion years to reach perhaps some form of intelligence wondering where that light came from.

While I ponder at the meaning of things that have no meaning, I risk missing the life that is before my very eyes at this very moment of time. I have what is here right now and that is what I celebrate. Life, whether it be mine, the aspen, the moose, the Steller's jay, the microbes filling every cup of seawater, is so precious. And even if it is not

unique in the universe, it is unique to what any of us will
ever see and experience. So we get to know the life we are
in, we look at it, we smell and touch it, we worship it since
it is what we have and all we will ever see. At least in the
here and now. Sometime in the future, or in some other life
or reincarnation of life, who knows. We sing praises to our
long removed ancestors who struggled to live in a world
they were part of. Maybe their atoms came from a passing
meteor or exploded star from billions of years ago. Maybe
we are simply the congealed dust of atoms that once sped
at the speed of light across a night sky of billions of years
in the past. Does it matter?

We can sit wherever we are and repeat the same as we
did yesterday, but it will be slightly different because each
of us will be a different person tomorrow and next year
and a billion years from now. Time is us. It is our past, our
present, our future. We are time and we are the universe.
We are all there is and all we will ever know. So celebrate
and sing praises of joy and wonder. Rejoice at that.

ROSE PETAL MOON

I watched with awe and wonder as the full, rose-petal red moon rose over the West Elk Mountains on its way to a total lunar eclipse. Such events are rare and once carried a magical and spiritual meaning to the ancient peoples who watched them, not understanding the simple science of what was happening. I understood the science, and still found it magical and spiritual.

A few clouds wafted over the rising moon, giving it an ethereal and mysterious look, a hide and seek that somehow made it more significant. I lie on the ground, looking up into a sky hiding its polka dot painting of stars and galaxies, but now flicking on like someone flipped a switch as the sky darkened from the fading moon. What did those people of ten thousand years ago think of this sight? Did they think the world was ending? Surely events like this lingered in the stories from their ancestors. But their lives were simpler, with more magic and myth, associations made with coincidences and symbol. I wondered what their emotions were.

I soon lost that question as I tried to understand what my emotions were. Eclipses, of both sun and moon, have been occurring since the earth coagulated out of stardust and the moon formed from that supposed collision with some other large body long before any life struggled on this mass of rock later to be called Earth. What did it mean? Not the science of shadows and trajectories, but the fact I am a passenger and participant of some grand cosmic episode. Earth, and the moon, and the sun, and our contingent of billions upon billions of things are floating around in our universe. Time and space and life.

If the fact that I lie watching that heavenly light show wasn't spiritual enough, I realized that yes, this eclipsed all religions and dogma that have appeared since we fell out of the trees on the East African savannah hundreds of thousands of years ago. This was magic, this was spiritual, this was a miracle. And as this happened, how many of us were totally ignorant of its passing as we sat transfixed in front of modern technological devices or stayed inside doing whatever we do to avoid thinking about life and the universe.

Time passes, time repeats itself, time watches as new stars are created, old ones explode into oblivion, creating new stardust that someday, if time continues on its apathetic journey to some distant end, will coalesce into another Earth which may allow another one or two questioning souls like me to wonder about a red moon, as its sun casts a shadow that makes people cringe in fear or shout in amazement. Just as I find wonder in the geological process of earth rocks, where mountains are created, erode into sand, which forms rocks, which then rise to form new mountains, I realized this same process occurs in the night sky.

Time not only plays magic on this planet, it also plays with miracles in the universe, on a time scale so much longer than what astounds me here on my home planet. Back to that old thing called time.

As I lay transfixed by the sky spectacle, I thought I could have been lying here thousands of years before. I would be watching the moon disappear as would (if they were paying attention) the mastodon, the giant bison, the ground sloth. A great horned owl could have hooted off in the distance, as he just now did. Would he be unaware of the moon, other than this bright night light slowly dimming? I was time traveling again, as I have a tendency to do.

But then, I was suddenly brought back to real time as a freight train four miles away, down in the valley, let loose with its mournful whistle. When I was a youngster, longing for things still undreamed of, that lonely whistle first sounded a mile distant when the train slowed to go through town, then rose in volume then faded into the distance. That was the sound I heard as I lay thinking of the moon and time and how time changes yet doesn't change life and memories. As the train slowly headed east, it faded from my consciousness. Then I was back with the mastodons and the distant glaciers grinding away mountain tops, all while a rose red full moon slowly crept skyward as it had been doing for eons.

The darkness, tinted rose red, was eerie. Soon, the brilliance would return, enough I could walk my trails in bright moonlight. How could someone not be awed by this passing mystery? The moon was the same, showing the faces and splotches and whatever an imagination could see in those grayish rock and moondust plains and mountains that lie unchanged since the dinosaurs. But they should not be rose petal red. Some called it blood red but I didn't like the connotations. Blood would never fall on the surface of the moon, nor would rose petals ever bloom there, but either way, I liked the blossom of life over the idea of blood, even though blood is the life force of me and all that walks, flies or swims.

The silence of the night returned, along with an occasional hoot of the owl and the still chirping of the crickets, hanging on long into an autumn night. I felt

I could lie out there all night, contemplating the stars,
which were now in full blossom with the full moon
dimmed to darkness. The Milky Way exploded in speckled
profusion. The constellations, or as much of them as I
knew, beckoned me as they have called to explorers and
wanderers since time began. The scene opened my mind
as a child's fingers would open a book. I questioned, I
imagined, I speculated, I looked for answers that didn't
exist. A night sky does that to you. A red full moon does
even more.

The experts said it would be years before we could
see a red full moon in total eclipse again. If I were even
around, I would be ancient, probably still trying to figure
out the meaning of such things. So I had to savor this
rare moment. But weren't all moments, lying in the dark,
looking up at a full moon, whether in eclipse or not,
red or brilliant yellow white, rare moments? Our time
under any moon is short, as measured by such things as
galaxies, super nova, sunsets, and sunrises. I felt the entire
universe was watching me, waiting for that aha moment
when I finally realized how much I was part of this grand
spectacle of life and stardust. I would keep watching,
waiting for that familiar moon to reappear.

BEGINNINGS

I have always been fascinated with endings and things long past. I was reminded recently that every ending once had a beginning. And with the focus on animals and the energy of where I now live, that means birth and young. As with the geologic forces, every life, every form had a beginning. I have mourned the end, as with the dead mountain lion, the dead great horned owl, and the eroding of mountains, carving of canyons, drying of oceans. Every life, every form that ends, creates the way for a new beginning. That is the cycle of life, the circle of energy that long distant ancestors recognized more than we do today.

Within a couple months in this strange spring, with rain nearly every day in May, then blast furnace heat in June, we have had a parade of new life outside our front door. We had three wild turkeys nesting almost within a stone's throw of our house. Two hatched their chicks, then promptly left, not even saying goodbye to our worrying over them for weeks. But one afternoon, a new mother hen from a nest we didn't know existed came parading through the yard with her seven brand new chicks stumbling along behind her, cheeping and enjoying this new miracle called life. Then she left, not to be seen since. Did she, a proud new mom, bring them up the hill to show us?

We had a family of long-eared owls, a species we had never seen before, living in an area north of the Owl Pond which itself was next to a long time nest of great horned owls, vacant ever since the tragic death a few years ago of mama owl. We played hide and seek daily for a week, trying to get pictures of the young long-eared. They loved the area since they were there every day. They flew low, were long and sleek, unlike the large great horned. Then they left, content to explore their world. They were not afraid of us and would sit on a low branch of a juniper just watching these strange two-legged creatures, a fascination in their new owl world.

We have been inundated with cottontail rabbits this year, including many young running through the yard, sleeping by the front door, probably a main reason for the abundance of owls, hawks, and unseen others, ready to feast on raw rabbit meat.

Then there was the mountain lion. In the middle of the day, Katherine saw a juvenile mountain lion in our lane bound into the neighbor's field. My first thoughts were that mama lion kicked out junior, now ready to be on his own and out from under mom's paws. This idea was confirmed the next morning when our neighbor called to say she saw three mountain lions just a couple hours after our viewing and a half mile to the west. Since the big cats do not usually travel in the open, nor in a group of three, in the middle of the day, this was the only explanation.

The next day, looking out our front window mid-afternoon, I saw a deer fawn, which I guessed was less than a week old, walk into our lawn, look around, and slowly wander down the hill. No mama in sight, which worried me that maybe the young big cat had feasted on her. A couple days later, I again saw junior in the open field, exactly where Katherine saw big cat days before. Again, no mama in sight, although I knew that does were never far from junior, although often hidden and unseen. The next day, we saw a doe come by the front yard, but by herself. I wondered if this was mama, and if so, where was junior. Minutes later, we were treated to mom nursing junior just outside the kitchen window. Relief! Mom and baby were safe and enjoying this new life. Then the next day, in that same spot, I observed a doe with twins frolicking along beside her. Was this the same doe and fawn? I wondered if it was a second doe coming by to show off her newborn. If it was, and it could well have been, it staggered my belief that all these mothers or offspring were coming by to say hello.

With the plethora of new nuthatches, robins, finches, grosbeaks, and hummingbirds flying and fluttering near the house, we have been treated to new life in abundance this spring. But was it more than just chance encounters of the deer and turkeys coming into our yard? Were they indeed coming by to say hi? We want you to see this new life, this miracle of creation. Give us your energy and we will give you ours. Who has more to give? They certainly brighten my world and I hope I can offer them safety in theirs. It is theirs after all and I am just a visitor who leaves them alone and keeps them safe as much as I can.

Not having children ourselves, we did not go through the emotions of raising our own offspring. I have always tended to be more interested in animals other than human, so I find the miracle of animal birth more exciting. With humans, we have all the modern medicine and technology working to save every newborn. With animals in the wild, they are surviving as nature intended, struggling to evade being eaten by predators, or predators struggling to find enough to feed the young. The weak don't survive; the strong do, and pass on those traits that allowed them to make it. Humans have lost this basic law that Mother Nature passed down through the ages.

So when I worry that the big cat might get the deer fawn, the doe has that in mind as well. They have survived so far and I wish them well, but I also know that the cat needs a deer to eat in order to survive. Which one do I root for? That doesn't matter since nature takes care of the choice.

The beginning is a miracle, but life itself is the real miracle. The baby rabbit, the newborn fawn, the juvenile cougar who suddenly has to fend on his own, these all are the continuation of the circle of life that has formed a web so intricate, we mere humans have yet to fully understand how it works. As John Muir so simply stated, "Everything is hitched to everything else in this universe." How true. We break one single strand in this web, it unravels in ways so subtle, we may not even notice until it is too late. If I were to interfere and do something to ensure the fawn does survive, I have caused changes unknowable. But what I can do is enjoy the new life and wish it all well, and think about what this world means to that newborn life. I gain an unmeasurable energy as I see the fawn jumping and frolicking, as I listen to the young red-tailed hawk soar the heavens behind its mother, learning to hunt, to cry in fierce defiance of the world, giving notice to all prey below that he is hunting and is looking to eat those that are not paying attention.

It is not possible for me to marvel at the eroded red sandstone cliffs unless I see the sands stretching endlessly, slowly building up what will become rock. I cannot mourn the dead owl or mountain lion without realizing a new owl and lion will soon take its place. Whenever an ending does not create space for a beginning is when we all start that death spiral that will end in oblivion.

Buffalo Jumps and Lighted Candles

The Vore family settled the empty plains of northeastern Wyoming in the late 1800's, raising cattle where only a few short years before, vast herds of bison covered the endless grasslands. Lakota, Cheyenne, Arapaho, Absaroka, and other people had hunted them for centuries, basing their entire way of life on the Tatanka. But when the bison were killed off by the encroaching white invaders, the natives silently disappeared as well.

In the late 1960's, the current Vores, Woodrow and Doris, loved the land and regretted the fact that a new Interstate Highway 90 was scheduled to cross the southern edges of their ranch. Prior to construction, they would sit next to a large depression in the ground where the highway was surveyed to cross. They knew there was something special about this sinkhole and told the highway engineers they should not fill in and cross this depression. The engineers agreed and moved the highway a few yards to the south, making a broad curve to avoid the sinkhole. The Vores went to the sinkhole one last time before the big earth movers arrived, sat on the edge, speaking in soft voices to whatever they felt was special about this site. They knew something had happened here and a special energy radiated into the endless Wyoming skies.

As part of the construction project, the highway builders had archeologists excavate the depression so they knew exactly what was next to the big freeway. What they found became one of the premier archeological sites of the region. This sinkhole, about 200 feet in diameter and nearly fifty feet deep, was a buffalo jump. According to Cheyenne elder William Tall Bull, starting around 1500 AD, give or take a generation or two, the native inhabitants of the plains discovered a better way to buy their groceries. They herded a bunch of bison together and ran them over a cliff. Bodies piled up, hunters killed the animals that didn't die in the fall, they carved up the meat, prepared the hides, and used all parts of the animals. It was a smart move that helped them survive a little easier since their entire culture relied on the bison to furnish food, clothing, shelter and medicine. In a period of over 400 years, over 20,000 bison left their bones at the bottom of this pit, now buried by centuries of erosional deposition from the sides of the hole and from the dust from the rest of Wyoming. Modern archeologists rave about this wonderful example that can teach them so much about the people who remain only as distant spirits of this grassland.

At an archeological conference in the early '90s in Spearfish, South Dakota, only a few miles from the site, several speakers told of this discovery. They were interested in the usual scientific details, such as the number of bones, species of animals, spear points and other details. Tall Bull then spoke to the audience from the heart and without notes about his perceptions of modern archeologists. He raised a new consciousness in me about the whole idea of interpreting the past. He told of his ability to go to a site and visit with the spirits of his ancestors. He saw the trails left by blue lights and visions essential to his religion. He could follow the energy of his elders. His message was that we are leaving out such an

important piece of history and fail to understand what
we are seeing. We must consider the spirits of his people.
His ancestors lived here for thousands of years in total
harmony with the land. He agreed with the conclusion
of modern environmentalists that we needed to tie in the
human aspect with the scientific details.

Tall Bull explained how a people and a civilization can
live as part of an environment. He gave visions of hope,
shattered though they are, in speaking of an environment
now alien to that which nurtured his ancestors. He brought
to life what we have destroyed, and what we are ignoring
in even trying to interpret this past. I thought later that
Tall Bull may be an ancient Cheyenne counterpart of
Jerry Falwell, a fundamentalist spirit- (rather than Bible-)
thumping zealot. Maybe so, but his message made sense
to me. He spoke from a saddened heart of something we
cannot really understand. He spoke mysticism, about those
blue lights turning into owls, about bison who came to
the call of his people. He spoke about a respect he and his
people had for all other forms of life, for the Tatanka who
sustained his people, to the earth that sustained them all.

Then that very same night that I learned of the buffalo
jump from Tall Bull and others, I watched the annual
Peter, Paul, and Mary Christmas Concert on PBS. Idols of
mine for decades, Peter, Paul, and Mary were unmatched
in the unabashed hope (as well as sadness) they evoked
in their songs. They symbolized the hope raised briefly
during the revolutions of spirit of the 1960s. "Blowing in
the Wind," "Where Have all the Flowers Gone," "If I Had
a Hammer," all served to give life, however briefly, to the
good that we are capable of doing as well as undoing. The
idealism of the '60s, so tragically buried by years of greed
and ignorance, made me wonder indeed, where had all

the flowers gone. Did anyone care anymore about a future where sharing and caring and goodness and goodwill still lived? How could I relate this to the buffalo jump?

As they pounded out hope and goodness of human potential they sang about lighting a candle and encouraged us to not let the light die out. The camera panned the children in the choir who held lighted candles, as did many in the audience. A song about hope, and the children that hope is entrusted to, made me realize that all the events of that day did indeed tie together. They tied the meaning of the past with the tragedy we have made of the sacred earth, and the hope that we can still do right by the spirits of William Tall Bull's ancestors.

The Cheyenne and Shoshone, Absaroka and Arapaho lived for thousands of years as part of their world. They were a part of a system that ran in harmony; they saw the earth as their mother and their provider. They evolved a religion that taught them to respect the bison they killed for food and they had traditions that their shamans kept alive. They realized their limits and their bounds but their spirits did indeed ride the winds and protect the buffalo jumps. William Tall Bull was saddened that we not only didn't care about the spirits, we were ruthlessly destroying them in our arrogant attempt to interpret the past to fit our beliefs, not to mention that our lifestyle was destroying our very future.

We might never return to the respect that the Cheyenne showed for Mother Earth, but we could at least stop destroying our very air, water, and life itself. If we didn't stop, the children holding the candles and singing about keeping the light shining would have no reason to sing. Their candles would be blown out by the blizzards of dust as our Mother Earth sighed her last breaths, at least for our descendants. The spirits that protect the Vore Jump would have no future to protect. Their past would be a dead past. It may be already.

———•◆•———

A short time after my first visit to the site, I added the buffalo jump to a program I was doing featuring a walk under a full moon once a month. On a frozen January evening, over two dozen people braved sub-zero temperatures to hike down into the bottom of the depression to hear a short talk about the site. As I stood on the top waiting to escort any latecomers to the bottom, I played a cassette tape of wolf howls. The echoes of the wolf bounced off the fog descending in a thick mist. That same moment, while the wolf cries were fading, I heard the honking of geese from a low flying formation of Canada geese overhead, framed by a fog shrouded moon. I knew then that the blue light spirits of Tall Bull were telling us something. Maybe it had something to do with lighting a candle and keeping a spirit alive.

We need to keep the candles lit. We need to not only heed the warnings espoused by many today, we need to change our whole attitude. We need to sit by the edge of a buffalo jump in the full moonlight and listen to the spirits. We may not see the spirits that William Tall Bull could see, but we can feel them. Just listen to the story that the Vores told of their feelings sitting by the hole in the ground—they knew something was there. There are spirits among the bones of the bison and the wolves and the grizzlies. They are there among the nearby but still hidden bones of the mastodon. They are there floating in the buried aquifer that contains the meltwater of glaciers. They are there in

the protective blanket of snow that fell the day I visited
the jump for the first time. We must see and listen to the
spirits for they can guide the way to keep the light from
going out.

There has been hope and goodness expressed in the
smiles of the children singing their songs and chanting
to their guardian spirits. Shaman or not, there is magic
waiting for us to see. It will come to us whether or not
we listen to Peter Paul and Mary, whether or not we have
the opportunity to sit under a full moon at the lip of Vore
Buffalo Jump. We just need to open our eyes and see that
we are a humble part of what surrounds us, now and in
the past. And in the future to which lighted candles and
buffalo bones lead the way.

That is the spirit of a time and a hope called Christmas.
It is the modern religion of a St. Paul; it is the ancient
religion of Tall Bull. It is the sense the bison felt as they
and the mastodon and saber tooth cat slowly roamed the
plains avoiding the creeping advance of ice. It is hope for
the future, but it is also the lesson of the past. It is the
struggle to live every day with our neighbors and it is
thanks for the help we all give each other.

I'VE BEEN WAITING

I stand on the ridge top waiting. It seems like I have been waiting a long time, so long that I have to concentrate to think why I am waiting. I search the skies for an answer. The eagle soars overhead, far above, not much more than a black dot in the endless blue sky, a blue so bright, it hurts my eyes. The eagle has been playing in his sky for an hour. It is his sky since he owns it completely, something I could never hope to achieve. He flies low, hovering near the tree tops, then catches a thermal that sends him on a rising tide of air. His chirping sounds undignified, not the scream heard in movies, but something lesser. He doesn't worry about waiting for an answer. He doesn't even have any questions to ask, other than "where is my dinner?" He will find it; he always does. I continue to wait.

I watch the distant range of soaring rock and trees. The far off San Juan Mountains were once a sea of lava steaming and bubbling. They cooled to a deeply dissected and precipitous mass of eye-popping scenery which is the roof of the world, at least in this part of the world. If I could join the eagle and soar above them, I would scream in wonder. The mountains hold secrets unimagined by me or the eagle. They hide and nurture life, but stand sentinel each day as canyons and peaks, each sunrise and sunset in total apathy. They don't search for answers, they don't ask questions.

I watch the rocks at my feet. Once part of a mountaintop distant from here, they flowed along with the ice and water in a pulsing, rushing journey from high to low, gravity in motion. Someday, they, in the form of grains of sand, will reach their destination, a far off ocean that may not even be here on this earth right now. The world changes beneath their feet as they move, but their descent is unstoppable. It is all about time. They are covered now with lichens, grey, green, black, yellow. The lichens hitch a ride but notice no movement. They are part of what moves one grain of sand at a time as they eat the rock and dribble the crumbs.

Time is part of my question. How much time is there? When did it begin and where did it start? Time is what governs us all. It makes the eagle fly and it creates the wind that moves the treetops, stirs the waves that make the rain that erodes the mountain that carries the sand to the sea. You cannot touch time but it touches you; it touches me as I search for something, someone to ask my questions. I call to the chickadee but she laughs at me, returning my call from far down the hill, bouncing from tree to tree as she approaches closer to tease and taunt me.

Someone the other day told me again that I think too much, I ask too many questions. That is what the human species was designed to do, I reply. We weren't meant to sit back and accept what others do. We think, we challenge, we scream in protest, we don't let others intimidate us into silence and ignorance. But that means asking questions, probing, seeking. The deer don't ask, the junipers won't, the sandstone canyons can't, the seashore doesn't. The mountains fold and rise, then erode and disappear. The oceans move in constant motion, rise in clouds of vapor, whirl in hurricanes and winter blizzards, shape the land. But none of these asks one question. Yet, they are time, but maybe they don't care. They begin and end and move and stand still. I have to ask the question but I know there is no answer.

I stand on the ridge top and watch the sun sink into the western horizon. The clouds turn salmon, bright orange, pink, purple, then disappear into the blackness that hides the Milky Way. Somewhere out there, around another sun, circles a planet. Does someone stand there and look my way and ask a question? Maybe she has the answer I seek, and I have the answer she seeks. But I have no answers, only questions. Maybe that is the answer. There are no answers.

The eagle has landed for the night, the chickadee rests on a branch, the rocks cool off with the night chill. I walk down the ridge. Time has spent another day, but night time has begun, again, as it has for billions of years. Night is the chance to view the cosmos, where time rules supreme. The light of each sun has traveled at full speed for longer than any of us can comprehend. The interesting thing that Einstein brought to our attention is that there is no time on these speeding light photons. At the speed of light, beyond which nothing exists, there is no time. These photons that have traveled across the universe for billions of years are not one second older than when they left the boiling surface of a star long since blasted to uncountable atoms. Nothing of the star exists except as the rocks and oceans of a planet that coalesced around the remnants of the exploded star. But the photons created from the shining sun are still living in their own world that is still the non-existent star.

My god, I gasp, as I look from horizon to horizon and see nothing but darkness that is without limit. If the photon is timeless, then is the darkness between the photons timeless? Does the empty vacuum of the limitless space stay the same age as the photon that speeds through it?

I hear the hoot of the great horned owl. She is hunting, as she does every night in this darkness. She replaces the daytime eagle as if in a tag team match. She sees well enough to thrive on the mice and rabbits, who end their time becoming part of her, just as the atoms of the exploded sun become part of the planets. Life recycles in endless loops, timeless circles.

The darkness surrounds the quiet, hiding the secrets that taunt the daylight. Times flows as the sun circles the sky, but stops to watch the stars continue the journey. Why is this? Maybe because the endless time we see in the stars so stuns us with its immensity, we ignore it. We can see the progression of daylight time, the grass waving in the breeze, the grasshoppers and titmice living their lives, the clouds painting the sky. We cannot see the stars burning themselves to ash and gas.

I stand waiting. Waiting is watching time. I smile as I close my eyes. It is useless. Time seems to smile back. Time wins, it always does. Maybe I found my answers after all, I realize as I walk back down to the valley. It is dark, but I don't notice. Besides, I have all the time there is.

Interlude: Solstice 2008

Summer solstice, 2008.
Waiting. Foreboding in the air.
Something is brewing, has been for years.
Waiting. Life is changing. How?

Gas prices high and going higher.
Floods and tornadoes, hurricanes and earthquakes.
We can deal with these, acts of nature, Acts of God.
I can feel it, a growing mantra of anticipation, spoken
    with fear.

Some mystics say wait for 2012.
The Maya foretold it.
It is more cyclic, it is the Fourth Turning.
A regular cleansing; good times will emerge.

I feel something more. A silent rumble.
More cosmic, unforeseen. Unknowable.
Maybe they are coming to take us home.
Out there, somewhere. Or sometime.

There is no fear.
I think of the chant: turn out the lights, the party is over.
Are we over? Did we screw it up so bad?
Maybe it has happened before.

Did they come to take T. rex and his companions?
Did they do it wrong and are now watching us do the same?
The air is electric, besides being polluted.
Does the pollution increase the effect?

Solstice, the sun changes direction. Or so it seems.
The full moon wanes.
Mars has a visitor, scraping, violating.
Are we so effusive, we take our violence to other worlds?

Killing goes on in Iraq, in Afghanistan.
Starving continues in Sudan, in Bangladesh.
Myanmar is strangled by its own,
Pakistan hates us all.

The Dalai Lama preaches peace
The Pope lives in his irrelevant piety.
Our zealots, of all brands, cry out in sanctified hypocrisy.
I wonder when civilization will begin.

The sun still rises, slowly going south
As it has since time began.
The birds still fly, the chipmunk still scampers up the tree.
Maybe it won't change for them.

Interlude: Parallel Universes

Somewhere, sometime
I became lost. I fell into a time warp
Leaving all I knew, all I understood
Behind in some vaporous cloud.

I looked around in confusion,
Not recognizing things I thought I knew.
My memory was clear, places familiar.
But my values were alien to the rest of the travelers

I thought back to when we parted.
No clear break, just a muddle of change.
I left myself behind as I stepped across a threshold
Entering a universe nearly like mine.

But different in so many ways.
I recognized looks of dismay in old friends.
The newer friends were strangers.
They didn't know the world I knew.

It was they who were lost
I knew my way. I remembered the paths.
The songs were old friends. They took me back.
The world they took me to was gone.

I asked where had all the flowers gone.
A voice whispered they were blowing in the wind.
Someone called to me.
They said I know you are out there somewhere.

What is lost is found
What is found is unknown.
Our gaze searches for something familiar.
What we see is across a barrier, unreachable.

The voice said to look inward.
Just because it can doesn't mean it should.
Progress isn't measured in speed.
A light beam goes fast, we can't see it move.

Some things are too fast.
Passing us before we notice.
They say the good things take time,
Aging like fine wine.

Understanding must mature.
It grows and feels it's way.
The facts may change,
The consequences may not.

The sky looks the same,
But the stars have moved just a little.
I can tell when the mountains move.
I can't tell when the universe shifts.

So rather than admit I'm out of touch,
I call it something larger.
A cultural revolution, a generational change.
That takes the responsibility away from me.

I'm still in charge of my universe.
I am comfortable with it, an old friend.
Warm and fuzzy as a puppy.
My security blanket.

If your world has left mine,
that is not my fault.
I still wonder where the fault line is.
As major as the San Andreas, it should be visible.

I cannot see it, cannot feel it.
But the gap is widening.
I won't try and step over.
I will ride it to the stars.

Enjoying the color of my trees,
the smell of my flowers.
I shall listen to my music
And dance to my rhythm.

I don't mind if you get out of step, sing out of tune.
I love my universe and will ride it to the edge of sight.
The stars are brighter, the breeze gentler.
Time slows to a crawl. My smile never stops.

The Stories Behind the Stories

*Stop and look at things that no one else has
bothered to look at. This simple process of focusing
on things that are normally taken for granted
is a powerful source of creativity.*

Edward de Bono, *How to Have Creative Ideas*

---

*In order to be open to creativity, one must
have the capacity for constructive use of solitude.
One must overcome the fear of being alone.*

Rollo May, *Creativity*

Behind The Stories

Each essay or poem often had a complex and interesting history behind it. The writing took place on scene, or in some cases, months or even years later, after much reflection and remembrance. This is the second book in a collection of the essays and poems I have written over many years. When I decided to write the first book, *Canyon Breezes* (Lichen Rock Press 2015), I chose writings that reflected more on nature and places in nature. I selected another group of writings that reflect more on my musings about time; those are the ones in *Zephyr of Time*.

Zephyr of Time. I have ridden the California Zephyr, a West Coast to Chicago Amtrak train, three times in my life. All three times played a significant part in my history. The first trip was to return to my home in Illinois after my first visit to the Colorado Rockies as a young boy. That trip changed my life since I was hooked on the mountains and the West after that. The second trip was to return to my boyhood home for my parents' 50th wedding anniversary. The third was to return to Illinois to clean out the house I grew up in after my father's death. That trip ended my ties with my home and youth.

I equate the word "zephyr" with these trips into my memory. When I decided to make my second book about time-related writings, I thought about the word zephyr and how it related to my past. Now past the age of Medicare, I know my time on this earth is more behind me than ahead of me. The gentle west wind called the zephyr described the call of the West that drew me away from my Illinois home to spend the rest of my life in or west of the Rockies. The zephyr pulled me both ways throughout my life.

Who Owns Time. Because I moved my permanent residence, along with everything I owned, seventeen times after I began my career with the Forest Service in 1970 (not counting the nine temporary homes between high school graduation and starting my career), I have always felt a vagabond, without a permanent place to call home. Of course the house I grew up in remained in Central Illinois until that day in 2002 that I drove away, leaving it forever. It and my parents were always there, although my life had moved West. When my second parent passed, the realization hit me like a brick—I was now totally on my own on this earth, without that security blanket called a parent.

Since by this time Katherine and I had a house and home we intended to remain in for the remainder of our lives, it felt finally like a home—our home. Because of the circumstances of ownership, I could easily identify the very few owners of this piece of property. But the land has been here much longer and that history belongs to me as well.

Blowing in the Winds. When I decided to combine the concept of time and the zephyr west wind, I needed to tie the two together in my evolving philosophy of life. This was my attempt, relating past experiences to the blowing winds.

Time. On one visit to my ninety-something-year-old father, he asked me this question: what is time? That question floored me. Not the question itself, but the fact he asked it. He and I never had a close relationship—that didn't happen in his generation. One of thirteen children, he was not that close to his father and his attitude carried over to us. I respected him and I knew he was proud of both his sons, but he and I rarely had significant discussions like this. After my mom passed, his life simplified to things like watching Lawrence Welk and reminiscing with his good hunting buddy about the old times chasing coons through river bottom woods. Afterwards, I reflected more and more about his question and how I could have answered him. I kept my answer to him simple. My thoughts on time itself are not so simple

Miracles on a Timeless Seashore. I had several references to seashores scattered through several essays. They seemed out of place. I pulled them together, added more thoughts and this essay resulted. To a landlocked mountain dweller like myself, the seashore has a special calling. I have only been on the ocean three times, none of them sailing out of sight of land. To me, the ocean itself would be boring. The seashore combines the mystique of the endless ocean with the land I am familiar with. It defines a struggle of the two major forces on this earth— land and water. The word miracle is often related to religious happenings. For me, the seashore is a miracle, since that is where the original life on earth left the sea and climbed onto land. It is a synthesis of both worlds.

Time Machine. I have always been fascinated with the concept of time. It was the subject of my first novel, *The Sands of Time* (unpublished as of 2016), in which time travel was a major topic. Although I have wished and fantasized about going back in time, I have never been interested in going forward into the future. I have spent a great deal of effort in trying to figure out how quantum physics (as much as I or anyone else can really understand it) deals with the concept of time.

Santa Fe Night. During my fire assignments after my retirement from active Forest Service duty, I often found myself in situations with nothing important to do. This happened on an assignment in Santa Fe in 2005. I was prepositioned there in case the big one hit. Both the Forest Service and Park Service had requested me, but they struggled to keep me busy. Thus I wrote to fend off boredom.

The Quarry. Soon after I retired from the Forest Service and moved to our new home in Delta County, Colorado, I saw a notice in the newspaper about an open house at the Dry Mesa Quarry. Katherine and I drove the two hours to get to this remote spot on the Uncompahgre Plateau. Being interested in geologic time and the geology of the Colorado Plateau, I was intrigued by this site.

Another Day in Paradise. For several years, Katherine and I made one or two trips to the Moab area each year. We found several favorite places off the beaten path and spent time wandering through this slickrock paradise. On one trip, we discovered a place overlooking the Colorado River basin south of Moab. On this trip, we were intrigued not by the fantastic scenery, but by the human history. Obviously not the first person to stand on this spot, I wondered what one of the first would have thought. Most likely not much in common with what I was thinking.

The Trestle. When I was transferred to Sierraville on the Tahoe National Forest in 1984, I lived in a temporary rental for a few weeks at White Sulphur Springs resort outside Portola, California. Katherine remained at our house in Grass Valley until we bought a new house and tried to sell the old one. During evenings after work, I would explore the forest near my rental house. This was called the East Side of the Sierra, much different from the wetter West Side. The forest was mostly Jeffrey pine and had been heavily logged at the turn of the century. Because the country was relatively flat, most logging had been by loggers using railroads rather than roads. The forest had mostly grown back, with large old yellow barked Jeffreys still dominating the pine and fir forest. There were traces of old narrow gauge railroad tracks or rights-of-way over much of my new ranger district. I happened upon a hidden trestle and jotted down these thoughts.

Aging Campgrounds. In 2007, I was starting to reflect more on my age and my past. Katherine's mother had dementia and we had finally put her in a nursing home. We purchased a 'new' used travel trailer in which to make the trip to California to visit, probably for the last time. Before embarking on the long trip with a new trailer, we made a test run to Colorado National Monument outside Grand Junction. We stayed in the National Park campground and these were my thoughts about camping in luxury, something I would have never thought would happen when I first started my career forty years earlier.

Of Brambles and Old Fences. We purchased the
Colorado property in late 1990. We intended to retire here
in 2002 when I turned fifty-five. By 1997, I had enough
of the rapidly changing Forest Service and retired early.
My new full time job was cleaning up the old homestead
where Hazel, the recluse had lived for over fifty years. The
place was a mess and in those early days I reflected a lot
on Hazel, her life, and why she lived as a complete hermit,
shutting out the world. I intended to write a book about
her and her life here, but hit a brick wall. None of her old
neighbors knew much about her. I couldn't gather enough
facts to write anything. She was a mystery woman. I ended
up writing a historical fiction novel, using what I knew of
her life, but I also wrote many essays about her and her life
here. We finally tore down her old log cabin in 2003 and
built a new log building. The clean-up for this took years.
There are now very few traces of Hazel and Walt, but I will
never forget her, even though I never met her in person.

Byron's Flower. This essay is self-explanatory, based on a
book I found at a library used book sale in Paonia. I wrote
a short story based on my fictionalized explanation of the
writing in the book. I have a habit of making up a fictional
story when I don't know the actual facts. Life can be fun
doing this.

Methuselah. This resulted from another one of my boring
fire assignments. I was a one-person fire information team
stationed in the Mendocino National Forest Headquarters
in Willows, California over the Fourth of July, 2008. I wrote
this after one afternoon when I experienced a very old

man who visited the Forest Centennial Open House. There were several forest fires going on, but my assignment in the Supervisor's Office didn't allow me close contact with any of the fires. I was there to assist the Forest Public Affairs Officer, but things quieted down while I was there. I wrote this on July 4, while sitting in the office, with no phone calls or anything else to do.

Prairie Thunderstorm. While putting together a book about my youth, I tried to remember some of the events of my childhood growing up in small town central Illinois. This was one of my remembrances of a time long ago.

Mendocino. During the same fire assignment in which I wrote the essay "Methuselah," I wrote this poem. I was stationed on the Mendocino National Forest and I researched the meaning of the word Mendocino, which was attached to a lot of things in Northern California. The temperatures outside during my stay in July were 115 degrees. I pitied the firefighters out on the firelines, glad I was in an air conditioned office and staying in an air conditioned motel. I wasn't always this lucky on my fire assignments.

Autumn. When I walk the trails on my property in Colorado, I am usually by myself. My mind never stays still, thinking of what I am seeing or whatever I happen to think about in my stream of consciousness rambles. Changes in the seasons usually make me think of past and future and changes soon to happen.

The Grave. Wherever we lived, we explored the country around us. This included Colorado, California, Utah, South

Dakota, and adjoining states. Managing thousands of acres of National Forest allowed me to explore in detail the lands I managed. Weekends found us exploring these as well as other locations. While in Northern California, we found one location outside of Portola that included an old falling down homestead as well as a small cemetery. Even though it was most likely private land, it was remote and uninhabited. To me, the landownership in a setting like this meant nothing. The spirits owned this.

New Year's. I have not celebrated holidays for years. This includes Christmas, New Year's, birthdays, etc. One New Year's Eve, I penned my thoughts on the upcoming day of celebration for many.

The Root Cellar. As I mentioned above in "Of Brambles and Old Fences," I have a whole book of writings on Hazel and the property we purchased in 1990. I wanted to write a non-fiction historical account of Hazel and her neighbors of a Redlands Mesa now changed beyond recognition. I got to calling this place during Hazel's time "a little Appalachia." During the Depression and years after, this area included mostly subsistence farmers, all living on the edge and squeaking out an existence. My limited knowledge of Hazel herself was full of fascinating stories and contradictions. However, I could find very few old timers who could tell me much about her. The most common answer, even from her next door neighbors was "we really didn't know anything about her." She was a recluse who shut out the world around her and would have taken after me with a shotgun if she knew I would be probing her private life. I still intend to finish my historical novel based on Hazel.

Christine's Story. When we moved to South Dakota from Utah in 1992, the drive to reach our property, which eventually became Cedars Retreat, was lengthened to twelve hours. So when we came south, we now spent a week, instead of the weekend when we lived only five hours away in Utah. One of the two routes we usually took went through Wyoming and Rawlins. The first time through, we stopped for our lunch break in the cemetery at the edge of town. It was a green tree-shaded spot after hours of desolate but beautiful Wyoming plains. This was the story I discovered.

The Cemetery. After retiring and moving to Colorado in 1997, I spent a lot time exploring my new and final home. I have always been interested in the local history of wherever I lived. This 1999 essay was the result of my discovery of some of the past history of Hotchkiss,

Tragedy at the Owl Tree. As described in my earlier book *Canyon Breezes,* I had discovered a dead mountain lion only a hundred yards or so downstream from the Owl Tree. The Owl Tree had provided a wonderful nest for great horned owls for years. We always took parental pride in watching mama owl on her nest, then awaiting the first view of the fluffy new chicks. When we found the dead lion, it was a spiritual and sacred experience seeing a deadly predator dead herself. Then the owl. Although a smaller meat eater, the owl had its power and respect just as much as the lion. To see her dead, with chicks dead in the nest beside her, moved me to reflect on life.

Ending as Beginning. In a mournful and reflective mood, probably about the time I reached the age of Medicare, I thought about life.

The Last Passenger Pigeon. This chapter, starting with this essay, is personal for me. Of the several books I have written but not yet published, one is about growing up in my home town of Tuscola, Illinois. I have written many essays about my childhood and hometown, and also about my family and the past about which I knew only a small part. One year, I happened to be home when my dad had a dinner in his honor and presentation of his fifty-year Masonic pin. He had his picture taken with three older brothers, who had earlier received fifty-year pins. This event in itself was noteworthy, but what I realized as I looked at that picture years later was all the brothers were now gone. At that time, my dad was the last; he almost made it to year 97 for his lifespan. I began to wonder what it was like to be the last. I wrote in *Canyon Breezes* about my thoughts of what it was like for the last grizzly bear in Colorado. Now I likened my dad, as the last of his brothers, to the passenger pigeon, the last one named Martha who died in the Cincinnati zoo in 1914. My dad was nine years old when the last passenger pigeon died. What was it like to be the last one?

Route 36. US Highway 36 used to be a major national East-West highway that formed the southern edge of my hometown in Illinois. It proved to be significant in my life as it was the route that led me West. It was symbolic as the way to my future. After Interstate 70 was built, it took the place of the more scenic but much slower Route 36. Over the years on many trips back to visit my folks from my various homes in the West, we would occasionally leave I-70 and drive on bits and pieces of old US 36. I compared the demise of US 36 to the demise we all feel as we age and lose bits and pieces of our past. Driving on US 36 on this trip brought back memories and meanings. Life changes, some things disappear, new ones take their place. The meaning of Route 36 may not have the same meaning to anyone else. I found that sad, but I find that to be part of life and evolution. We all change, as does our world.

Homebound on the Zephyr. This was probably the saddest essay I have written since it dealt with the passing of my last parent and my journey home for the last time ever. This captures more than any other of my stories the meaning of time and the zephyr wind of change.

The Coon Tree. This is the first of two essays that I wrote to accompany drawings that Katherine did for my parents. Dad was a coon hunter who loved to spend winter evenings clambering through the river bottom woods near Tuscola, Illinois, in search of raccoons. He loved the hunt and didn't care about the result of his shooting. He let his coon hunter partners keep the coons for skins. He respected the raccoon and found it a worthy challenge. He finally got too old for the hunt, but spent his final years recounting endless stories with Bill, his last surviving hunting buddy. I heard all the stories many, many times. Katherine's drawing was of an old half-dead oak (she used an ancient black oak near our California foothill home for her *plein air* drawing) but I used artistic license to place the tree somewhere along a river bottom my dad was very familiar with. Again, I dwelt on the past and the loss of part of ourselves as time passes by.

Granddad's Barn. This was written to accompany a drawing Katherine did for my mother to honor a barn that her father used in his farming. I never knew any of my grandparents, but heard plenty of stories to picture them in my mind. At some point in the 1970s, my mother took us out to the still-standing barn so Katherine could do a drawing. Soon after that, the barn was torn down. After Katherine did the drawing years later I wrote this to go with it. Again, this is to honor a past that is gone forever.

Little Boy Blue. Eugene Field wrote the poem "Little Boy Blue" in 1888. My mother, during her early school days, copied the poem on a poster board and illustrated it with magazine pictures. I discovered it in the bottom of her cedar chest as I was cleaning out the house after my father's passing in 2002. Mom passed in 1993. I helped my brother clean out the house in order to sell it. The morning I discovered her childhood poster, I was alone in the house, surrounded by memories. As I read her poem, I totally lost it as emotions overwhelmed me. To this day, I still cannot read my poem without tears. It sums up my emotions about the past and the fact that those zephyr winds take us away from many things, never to see them again.

The Pictures. Carol, a high school classmate whom I have seen only a couple of times in fifty years since graduation, sent me some photos she had discovered hidden away. They were taken of her 4th grade class. At that time, I didn't know any of these kids since we went to different schools. I thought about what these kids were thinking in 1957 and what had happened in those ensuing decades. This was a time machine, taking us all back to that moment years ago.

Starry, Starry Skies. To me, the epitome of what time is all about is connected with sitting outside under clear

Western night skies, looking at the stars overhead. The unbelievable distances, the incomprehensible amount of time as represented by the journey of the light from these distant stars and galaxies overwhelms anyone who tries to think about what it all means.

Rose Petal Moon. The eclipse on September 27, 2015, was advertised and hyped to be a rare event. I had envisioned a full moon rising over Mt. Lamborn to be a worthy picture for the cover of this book. A full moon in total eclipse would be even better. I set up the telescope on the ground while Katherine sat upstairs on the deck with her camera, taking dozens of photos while I contemplated the view. It certainly would have been mystical and magical to someone thousands of years ago. It wasn't bad for me, either.

Beginnings. I tend to focus on the endings as represented by the passage of time. But the spring of 2015 made me realize that whatever ends also means something else begins. It seemed to be more than coincidence that we were overwhelmed by the young that roam our nature preserve. We take pride in the wildlife that find refuge and share their lives with us. Owls, rabbits, deer, turkeys, songbirds—they rewarded us more than normal this year with new life. Life is about birth as well as death. The two go together.

Buffalo Jumps and Lighted Candles. Two events came together for me nearly twenty-five years ago. I learned of the Vore buffalo jump and I listened to one of my perennial favorites, Peter, Paul and Mary sing on their annual Christmas special for PBS. I wrote this soon after the

election of 1992, which to me at least indicated a time of
hope. A man of my age and generation was ready to usher
in a time that my generation had worked for a quarter
century to achieve. The buffalo jump and the songs tied
this together.

I've Been Waiting. I have always sought answers and
solace in nature. Ever since I came out West in 1965, I
have stood alone on hilltops, canyon edges, valley or
river bottoms, forest thickets and desert expanses. I have
watched wildlife, trees, star filled skies, full moons, clouds
red from sunrises and sunsets. I have sought answers from
questions I could not even put into words. I have felt more
at home with the zephyr winds and the timeless expanse
of galaxies.

Solstice 2008. Solstices and equinoxes have special
meaning to me. I know they also did to aboriginal peoples
and cultures. Maybe I belong more to the Anasazi or Inca
than to my own age.

Parallel Universes. As I get closer to my eighth decade,
I feel more and more estranged from this world. I'm sure
my 96-year-old father felt the same way near his end. The
world has changed, but that is life. The theme of these
essays is change and time. Each of us lives and explores
life. Then, sometimes slowly, sometimes rapidly, we realize
life has changed and our time peaks, then passes. Just like
that elusive west wind. New lives come onto the scene and
they take their turn. We reflect and try to make sense.
Sometimes we can, often we cannot.

About the Author

Joseph Colwell has worked and lived across the West for half a century. During his college years at the University of Idaho, he spent summers working in Idaho state parks, Mt. Rainier National Park, and Grand Canyon National Park. With his degree in wildlife management, he spent the next 27 years with the US Forest Service, working on five different national forests, managing and exploring the land. As an ecologist and naturalist, he had many experiences in being close to nature. Retiring from his Forest Service career, he continued work on wildland fires as a Fire Information Officer, assisting the general public and homeowners in understanding wildfires.

Joseph and his artist wife Katherine now live on their 40 acre nature preserve overlooking the North Fork Gunnison River Valley of western Colorado. They created Colwell Cedars Retreat, which offers a peaceful secluded haven for guests as well as wildlife.

They can be reached at ColwellCedars.com.